DEADLINE EFFECT

"Cox is a seasoned dispenser of constraints and expectations, and, in turn, a coaxer and a cajoler of those who must meet them. . . . He wants to demystify deadlines in order to defang them, to assure us that if we just tilt our heads we can see our demons as our friends."

—Rachel Syme, *The New Yorker*

"Almost every page has the kind of information on it where you call out to whoever's in the room and say, 'Oh my god, did you know this?' It's full of easter eggs of anecdote and joy, on top of being a wonderful piece of thinking."

—Rivka Galchen, author of *Atmospheric Disturbances* and *Everyone Knows Your Mother Is a Witch*

"*The Deadline Effect* is an amazing read—it really hits home since I'm constantly on deadline. Fascinating stories and practical takeaways!"

—Julia Boorstin, senior media and entertainment reporter, CNBC

"When you have a healthy relationship with crunch time, the book argues, you can do great work *and* enjoy vacation to the fullest."

—*GQ*

"Christopher Cox is highly lucid and a quick learner, who also happens to be skilled at explaining big ideas through stories. The examples are wildly various and creative, and each features high stakes: will the Easter lilies be ready to ship on time? Will the new restaurant open on schedule? Will the box store be prepared for the crush of Black Friday? A wry and literate how-to, a counterphobic look at the deadlines we fear yet couldn't live without."

—Ted Conover, professor and director, Arthur L. Carter Journalism Institute of New York University

"In *The Deadline Effect*, writer and magazine editor Christopher Cox has set out to better understand the way we respond to deadlines, how they can at once be stressful and clarifying experiences, and if there's a way to trick ourselves into the latter without any of the former."

—*Lit Hub*, "Nonfiction Books You Should Read This Summer"

"In the eternal battle between human beings and the clock, Christopher Cox's *The Deadline Effect* offers a compulsively readable truce. In these seven vivid profiles of organizations under extreme stress, *The Deadline Effect* addresses a common conundrum with unusual insight. They say if you want something done, give it to the busiest person in the office but if you want to know *how* it gets done, give it to Christopher Cox."

—Sloane Crosley, author of *Look Alive Out There*

AVID

READER

PRESS

THE
DEADLINE
EFFECT

INSIDE ELITE ORGANIZATIONS
THAT HAVE MASTERED
THE TICKING CLOCK

CHRISTOPHER COX

AVID READER PRESS
New York   London   Toronto   Sydney   New Delhi

AVID READER PRESS
An Imprint of Simon & Schuster, Inc.
1230 Avenue of the Americas
New York, NY 10020

First Avid Reader Press trade paperback edition July 2022

AVID READER PRESS and colophon are
trademarks of Simon & Schuster, Inc.

For information about special discounts for bulk
purchases, please contact Simon & Schuster Special Sales
at 1-866-506-1949 or business@simonandschuster.com.

The Simon & Schuster Speakers Bureau can bring authors
to your live event. For more information or to book an
event contact the Simon & Schuster Speakers Bureau at
1-866-248-3049 or visit our website at www.simonspeakers.com.

Interior design by Lewelin Polanco

1 3 5 7 9 10 8 6 4 2

Library of Congress Cataloging-in-Publication Data has been
applied for.

ISBN 978-1-9821-3227-9
ISBN 978-1-9821-3228-6 (pbk)
ISBN 978-1-9821-3229-3 (ebook)

For Georgia

Contents

THE
DEADLINE
EFFECT

Introduction

In 2006, a US Census worker named Elizabeth Martin devised an experiment. Every ten years, the federal government is constitutionally required to count the number of people in each state, and every ten years it's a headache. Most of the census is conducted by mail, and it turns out that it's enormously difficult to get people to respond to detailed questions about their lives with little incentive other than a sense of civic duty.

If you live in one of the households that won't respond to the postal questionnaire, the government sends an "enumerator" to your address to conduct the count face-to-face. And that is an expensive undertaking, requiring a staff of hundreds of thousands to knock on millions of doors. Martin wanted to find out what she could do to improve the mail-in response rate to the 2010 census and take some enumerators off the street. Even a small improvement would make an enormous difference: for every percentage-point increase in the number of households responding, the government would save $75 million.

The Census Bureau had already tried a variety of tricks to get people to fill out the forms. They had tweaked the design of the questionnaire, added warnings about penalties for nonresponders, and sent a flurry of reminder postcards. Those all had a modest effect. But Martin, in her experiment, tried something simpler: give people less time to respond. The same questionnaire with the same census date—April 13, 2006—was sent to two groups of people, but one group got it a week later than the other.

She sent it out to more than 28,000 households, in all fifty states, and waited for the forms to come back. When they did, Martin saw that her hunch had paid off: it was the second group—the one with seven fewer days to work on the form—who had the higher response rate, by two percentage points. Even more significantly for a census employee obsessed, by necessity, with the quality of her data, the group with a shorter deadline made fewer errors in their responses. Implemented nationwide, the reliability of the census data would improve markedly. And, of course, there was the matter of those two percentage points—$150 million in savings, all from adjusting a deadline.

The results from the mock census were counterintuitive, but they didn't surprise me. I had conducted a similar experiment myself. A writer, John, was on the hook to write the cover story for *GQ*, where I was the executive editor. We had flown him out to Los Angeles to interview Diddy—also known as Puff Daddy—about a rumored new album. We also sent a photographer to shoot Diddy in a variety of fancy cars, hired a video team to make a behind-the-scenes short film, and sold advertisers on the whole package. It was a big production, and at the center of it all was John and the 5,000 words we had assigned him to write.

John was famous for blowing deadlines. He was reportedly

several *years* late on an assignment for *The New Yorker*. He was also an incredibly stylish writer, someone who could elevate almost anything (including, oh I don't know, an interview with a somewhat less than fully cooperative hip-hop legend) to the level of art. If you could get him to cough up a draft.

I had worked with John before, and it often required dozens of phone calls, countless emails, and a lot of anxious waiting to get him to start writing. We would plan for a story to be published in, say, the February issue, and inevitably it would have to be bumped to March or April or December.

But this time was different: because it was the April cover story, it couldn't be pushed to a later issue. The whole apparatus built up around the article would crash down if we didn't have a written profile of Diddy at the center of it.

So I lied to John. I told him that the absolute, drop-dead date to get the story in was a week before the actual due date. John, bless him, almost certainly knew I was lying, at least a little bit. No sane editor would ever tell a writer the actual deadline for a story. But he probably thought I was trying to buy myself an extra day or two, which is standard for editors negotiating with difficult writers. The trick in this case was giving him so little time to finish the story that he would start working on it immediately.

John wrote the article in a shared document, so I could see his progress as the dreaded date crept closer. Three days before the deadline: nothing there. Two days: still nothing. The night before, finally, a paragraph appeared, but then John started moving words around, fussing infinitely with the first six sentences but making no further progress. All the while, I was sending earnest and upbeat emails about how the finish line is just over the horizon! Eventually I went to sleep.

The next morning, I opened the document and there was a lot of text. A whole new section. And, thanks to Google Docs, I could see John's cursor, busily spitting out new words. I remembered what the playwright Tony Kushner told a reporter (for the *New York Times* Vows column, of all places) about his creative process: "I work best after the deadline has passed, when I'm in a panic."

My only regret was that I hadn't told John the deadline was even earlier. But that was being greedy. We still had a week, and John had already written thousands of words. Toward evening on deadline day, he sent me a message: "Close to complete draft. Please keep drawbridge down for 24 more hours. I won't let you down."

Sometime between the decoy deadline and the actual one we had something ready to be printed. I rushed it down to the production department and gave it to the fact-checkers. John returned to a blissful state of not-writing, Diddy climbed into his Maybach and drove away, and the April issue appeared as planned.

I already knew that a deadline was a force potent enough to break through even the worst cases of writer's block. But learning that setting a deadline early increased the chances it would be met—a finding replicated in studies far beyond the Census Bureau and the offices of *GQ*—was eye-opening. It promised, in essence, the productivity equivalent of the full-court press.

As an editor, I am professionally obliged to care about deadlines. The word itself, it's no coincidence, was adopted from the publishing business. The deadline was originally the line on a printing press beyond which no type could be set—though publishers in turn had borrowed the term from the military: during the Civil War, the "dead-line" was a boundary surrounding the stockade, outside of which any prisoner would be shot on sight. By the early twentieth century, the deadline came to mean not the physical limits on a battlefield or on a page but the hour a story was due.

The word was a great conceptual success, spreading to industries far beyond newspapers and magazines. It carries a sense of urgency and threat, which can be useful to all sorts of profit-driven and productivity-maximizing enterprises. Compare it with its near equivalent in French, *délai*, which can mean either deadline or delay, and you find a neat encapsulation of the differences between life in New York and Paris.

The Ancient Greeks, though, had the word that gets closest to the essence of a deadline. Most of us know the Greek word for ordinary time, *chronos*—the regular old drumbeat of existence, the flow of time that takes us from birth to death. But there's another word for time, *kairos*, which refers to the opportune moment, a time for decisions and action: the arrow drawn back and about to be released. Whereas the Greeks almost always depicted the god representing *chronos* as an old man, statues of *kairos* were youthful and sprightly. Aesop described him as bald, except for a lock of hair draped over his forehead: "If you grasp him from the front, you might be able to hold him, but once he has moved on not even Jupiter himself can pull him back."

It's that second conception of time, *kairos*, the opportune moment, that breathes life into a deadline. It also speaks to two ideas you'll find linked in this book. First, deadlines are powerful motivators—the god is young and vigorous. Second, deadlines can be manipulated—you can catch him, but only if you know how to go about it.

The evidence for the first notion is robust. Several years ago, the behavioral scientists Amos Tversky and Eldar Shafir set up a simple experiment. They offered students $5 for filling out a long questionnaire and returning it to them. One group of students had five days to complete the assignment; another had no deadline. The results were unambiguous: 60 percent of the students with a deadline returned the questionnaire and got their $5. Only 25 percent of those with no deadline finished the task.

In 2016, Kiva, a nonprofit organization that lends money to low-income entrepreneurs, ran a real-world demonstration of the same principle. Kiva wanted to encourage more small businesses to apply for their interest-free loans, but the process was time-consuming and difficult: potential borrowers needed to fill out eight pages of financial disclosures and business plans. Only 20 percent of the businesses that began an application online completed it.

That was when Kiva decided to run a test: they would send reminder emails to everyone who had started and abandoned an application. One group would get an email with a deadline to finish applying for a loan; the other would have no deadline. Kristen Berman, who wrote about the results for *Scientific American*, highlighted a potential pitfall of this approach: "If the process requires a small business owner to invest significant amounts of time, then adding a deadline should *decrease* the number of applicants. People just won't have time to fill out the forms and they would miss the cut off." But that wasn't what happened. The small businesses that received a deadline were 24 percent more likely to complete their applications. Time wasn't holding these companies back; it was motivation. Kiva began issuing a lot more loans.

Deadlines can encourage productive behavior. I'm sorry to report, however, that they have a dark side. They aren't only a magic trick that puts $5 in students' pockets; they can also draw time and energy toward themselves like a black hole. The problem is that as soon as you set a deadline, work tends to get delayed until right before time expires. There's a name for this phenomenon: it's called the deadline effect.

Economists and game theorists love talking about the deadline effect, usually in the context of two-party negotiations: a union and a corporation, say, trying to agree to a new contract. Two groups sit down at the bargaining table, and something strange happens. As one paper from a pair of MIT economists put it: "A firm deadline is often imposed upon negotiators in order to prevent them from dragging out the negotiations indefinitely. Ironically, such deadlines themselves sometimes entice parties to delay the agreement." The deadline effect is the curse that keeps transit workers and the city deadlocked right until the eve of the strike. It is the reason that so many settlements are reached "on the courthouse steps."

The academics who study the deadline effect generally agree that it's bad—it's mighty, but it's destructive. Last-minute deals tend to be worse for all parties than what might have been agreed to if both sides had more time, for the same reason that a term paper thrown together at the last minute will be worse than one completed well before the deadline and fastidiously revised.

The stakes, of course, can be even higher than that. In 1992, in an effort to speed up the approval process for new prescription drugs, Congress set deadlines for decisions by the Food and Drug Administration. The FDA soon had a backlog of drug applications to process—and approved a large number just before time ran out.

A 2012 study found that those deadline drugs were more likely to need additional safety warnings and more likely to be removed from the market. "Safety-based withdrawal is 6.92 times greater for a drug approved in the two months leading up to its approval deadline than for comparable drugs approved at other times," the authors wrote. "These post-market events are associated with tens of thousands of additional hospitalizations, adverse drug reactions, and deaths." Congress had a smart plan—they used a deadline to get the FDA to act quicker—but they didn't account for the consequences, as the new rules pushed decisions to the last minute and rushed the agency's risk assessments.

The frustrating thing about organizations such as the FDA that fall prey to the deadline effect is that it's preventable. Many organizations have learned how to take the urgency a deadline provides and jettison all the down-to-the-wire nonsense. They are all master deadline manipulators: they have learned how to work like it's the last minute before the last minute. This book will tell their stories.

It's time to bring up a word I've been avoiding so far: procrastination. After this introduction, the subject will hardly come up. That's not because the people you'll meet in the chapters that follow are not affected by procrastination. It's because this book is a book about organizations, and effective organizations, especially the ones I write about here, have come up with systems to defeat procrastination without changing basic human psychology. Still, to understand how deadlines work, we have to understand their evil opposite.

The first people to use the word *procrastination* were concerned with precisely that—good and evil, damnation and salvation. Procrastination was "the worst of Satan's Engines," Anthony Walker, the rector of Fyfield, wrote in a 1682 sermon. Walker was referring to a particular kind of delay, though: putting off repentance. Jonathan Edwards, the great American revivalist, took up the theme a few decades later, preaching, "How can you reasonably be easy or quiet for one day, or one night, in such a condition, when you know not but your Lord will come this night? And if you should then be found, as you now are, unregenerate, how unprepared would you be for his coming, and how fearful would be the consequence!" The title of that sermon was "Procrastination, or The Sin and Folly of Depending on Future Time."

Today our worries are more secular, but the scourge is the same. The psychologist George Ainslie described procrastination as "the basic impulse," a human flaw "as fundamental as the shape of time." A meta-analysis of research on procrastination by Piers Steel, a professor at the University of Calgary, suggested that as many as 20 percent of adults (and 50 percent of college students) consider themselves chronic procrastinators, and the problem is growing. It's also costly: a survey by H&R Block concluded that we overpay our income taxes by $473 million a year because we procrastinate in filing our returns.

The psychological mechanism of procrastination is well understood. It's not just that people don't like to do unpleasant tasks: if that were a controlling aversion, nothing would get done. The problem is that we are time-inconsistent and present-biased: we tend to underestimate both costs and rewards the further they are in the future, a process called hyperbolic discounting. Don't let the jargon confuse you: this just means that we exaggeratedly (hyperbolically) underestimate (discount) the value of future gains and losses. Thus the satisfaction of finishing a project (a future reward) stands no chance against the fun of playing hooky for a day. Likewise, the pain of getting a blood test done today looms larger than the possibility of going in for a physical in six months' time. Humans aren't the only ones with this affliction. Rats have been shown to prefer a delayed, larger shock over a smaller, immediate one. (I read this finding in a journal article called "Procrastination by Pigeons.")

Relatedly, we tend to overestimate how much time we'll have in the future, which leads to some surprising results when it comes to activities we'd normally have no reason to put off.

In a study called "Procrastination of Enjoyable Experiences," Suzanne Shu and Ayelet Gneezy compared tourists who spent two weeks in Chicago or London and residents who had lived in those cities for an entire year. The tourists, who couldn't fool themselves that they'd have more time in the future, had seen more of the cities' landmarks than the locals had.

The same miscalculation of time affected participants in another experiment Shu and Gneezy ran. They distributed coupons good for a slice of cake at a pastry shop. One set of coupons expired in three weeks; the other expired in two months. They surveyed the recipients and found that only half of those with a three-week coupon were confident they would use it, while more than two-thirds of those with the two-month coupon thought they would. In reality, 31 percent of the three-week coupons and a paltry 6 percent of the two-month coupons were redeemed. The cake-less 94 percent simply thought they'd have more time later.

There is a whole literature devoted to defeating these innate biases through some creative rearranging of our mental furniture. With the right mind frame, the right mantra, the right dose of willpower, these books argue, we can put an end to procrastination and step gleefully into a new, productive life. There's another approach, though, that doesn't put quite as much weight on the prospect of curing human fallibility. It's a way of amplifying our self-discipline by externalizing it.

In an essay called "Procrastination and the Extended Will," two philosophy professors, Joseph Heath and Joel Anderson, discuss how cognition is best thought of not as the firing of neurons in a vacuum, but as the interplay among our brain, our bodies, and the environment. They cite the example of multiplication: while few people can multiply three-digit numbers in their heads, almost all of us can do it on paper. "When trying to characterize human beings as computational systems," they write, "the difference between 'person' and 'person with pencil and paper' is vast."

The same goes for all endeavors that we tend to think of as purely mental. "The self-controlled person is usually seen as one who has a capacity to exercise tremendous willpower," Heath and Anderson write, "not as one who is able to organize his life in such a way that he is never called upon to exercise tremendous willpower." Self-discipline, in this telling, comes from establishing external checks on our behavior. Odysseus doesn't overcome the lure of the siren's song through virtue alone; he orders his sailors to bind him to the mast.

"There is not all that much we can do, using our 'onboard' resources, when it comes to controlling procrastination," Heath and Anderson write. "When one moves into the domain of the environment, on the other hand, especially the social environment, the set of available strategies becomes less restricted." Rather than white-knuckling our way through an onerous task, we can create structures to help us overcome our natural inclination to delay hard work. The good news is that we have already come up with an incredibly effective structure to solve the problem of our weak wills, and it doesn't require any maritime knot-tying skills: it is the deadline.

Recently, I came across the story of Évariste Galois, a nineteenth-century mathematician whose short, doomed life provides an extreme example of a deadline at work. From an early age, Galois was known to be brilliant. His innovations in group theory, a branch of algebra that Henri Poincaré described as "the whole of mathematics . . . reduced to its pure form," have kept mathematicians busy for almost two hundred years. The only problem was that, until the fateful intervention of a deadline, he couldn't get his ideas down on paper.

Galois was born in 1811, in a suburb of Paris. His father was the mayor of the small town where he grew up; his mother was responsible for his early education and evidently taught him well. It was in school that his troubles started. He was impatient with those who couldn't keep up with him intellectually. The Argentine writer César Aira, who wrote about Galois in his novel *Birthday*, said that in mathematics in particular, "the young genius had acquired the habit of executing all the intermediate steps in his head and thus arriving abruptly at the results." During an admissions exam for the École Polytechnique, which had the most prestigious mathematics program in France, he threw an eraser in the examiner's face.

He was forced to enroll at the inferior École Normale, where, almost entirely on his own, he began breaking new ground in the theory of polynomial equations. "I have carried out researches which will halt many savants in theirs," Galois bragged. When he tried to submit his work for publication, though, reviewers rejected it as incomplete. He had everything straight in his head, but he couldn't make other people see it. One paper he submitted to the Académie des Sciences was judged simply "incomprehensible": "We have made every effort to understand M. Galois's proofs. His argument is neither sufficiently clear nor sufficiently developed to allow us to judge its rigor."

While Galois was at the École Normale, he became active in revolutionary politics. In July 1830, Parisians took to the streets to demand an end to the rule of the Bourbon dynasty and King Charles X. Over "three glorious days," they stormed the Tuileries Palace and the Louvre, eventually forcing the king into exile. At the end of the year, Galois published a letter excoriating the director of the École Normale for not letting students join the protests. The school expelled him.

He spent the following year investing in radical causes in

Paris. "If a carcass is needed to stir up the people, I will donate mine," he said. He joined the Artillery of the National Guard, which was openly defiant of the new French king, Louis-Philippe. He spent time in prison for his republican activities, including a stint for supposedly threatening the king's life: at a banquet attended by Alexandre Dumas, among others, he had toasted Louis-Philippe while holding a dagger in his hand.

None of this left much time for mathematics. Working on his own, he began revising the paper he had submitted to the Académie des Sciences to make it more accessible to the judges. We could say that he was engaged in hyperbolic discounting of the value of writing his ideas down, or that he was present-biased toward the thrills of being a revolutionary, but really he was just a willful kid who thought he had all the time in the world to be a mathematician.

The end to this drama came in May 1832, one month after Galois was released from prison. On May 25, he wrote to his friend Auguste Chevalier that he was feeling distraught, though he doesn't spell out the cause: "How can I console myself when in one month I have exhausted the greatest source of happiness a man can have?" Four days later, he told Chevalier that he had been provoked into a duel, which historians have ascribed either to a political disagreement or to a fight over a woman, or both. In the hours before he went to meet his rival, he stayed up late into the night writing letters. He wrote short notes to his republican friends, telling them good-bye, for he was sure he was going to die: "Please remember me since fate did not give me enough of a life to be remembered by my country." But he spent most of the evening feverishly writing a long letter to Chevalier.

"My dear friend," he began, "I have made some new discoveries in analysis." What followed was page after page of all the theoretical leads Galois had developed during his lifetime but neglected to follow, a last will and testament for the mathematical mind that would die with him. He annotated the papers he had submitted to the Académie. He wrote out new proofs and corrected others. Everything in these papers, he told Chevalier, had been clear in his head for over a year. His writing grew frantic as the clock ticked down. In the margin of one page he wrote, "There are a few things left to be completed in this proof. I have not the time." He closed his letter to Chevalier with a request to send his work to two of the leading mathematicians in France, so they could attest to the importance of what he had discovered: "Later there will be, I hope, some people who will find it to their advantage to decipher this mess."

The duel was fought at twenty-five paces, with pistols. Galois was shot in the stomach and collapsed. His seconds either abandoned him or went looking for help; in any case, a passing farmer discovered him and brought him to a nearby hospital. His brother Alfred was the only family member to make it to his bedside in time. "Don't cry," Galois told him. "I need all my courage to die at twenty." He was buried in an unmarked grave.

Galois's theories took decades to be properly deciphered and understood, but they now form an indispensable part of our understanding of mathematics. In 1951, the theoretical physicist Hermann Weyl marveled at the near-miss quality of it all, and the good fortune that Galois managed to get a final message to his friend: "This letter, if judged by the novelty and profundity of ideas it contains, is perhaps the most substantial piece of writing in the whole literature of mankind." For poor Galois, though, wouldn't it have been better if he found a different source of motivation than imminent death?

Évariste Galois and the overworked employees of the FDA have something in common: they were subject to a deadline they could not control. This is the worst form of the deadline effect—you may get the job done, but you're miserable. With a small amount of strategic thinking, however, you can change the way the story ends.

This book seeks to reclaim the deadline effect, to make it a term meant to describe successes rather than failures. To do that, I looked for examples of organizations that had developed a form of "extended willpower": systems meant to keep projects on schedule without sacrificing quality. After all, there's nothing inherent in the deadline itself that requires that trade-off. As one study from Hebrew University put it, "When the time for doing something—be it completion of a project or group decision making—is limited, people are less wasteful, and more focused, productive, and creative." It's a liberating realization: excellence and timeliness are not at odds.

I studied nine different organizations as they approached a high-pressure deadline to see how they handled it. In most of the cases, I was there right as the clock ticked down to zero. My rules for selecting these workplaces were simple: I wanted to cut across multiple industries, and the deadline in question had to be the biggest one of the year, or of multiple years.

Over the next seven chapters, you will see incredible feats: a restaurant opening for the first time, a crew covering a whole mountain in snow, a passenger jet rolling off an assembly line. You'll find out how a particular variety of white lily ends up in stores every year at Easter, and you'll go backstage at a theater before opening night. You'll embed with an Air Force squadron preparing to provide hurricane relief, a Best Buy on the eve of Black Friday, a robotics startup introducing itself to the public, a presidential campaign on the road to the Iowa caucuses. These organizations had many differences, but they were united in two ways: they took deadlines seriously, and they set up their operations so that no individual ever faced the ticking clock alone.

In many cases, it was the rank-and-file workers rather than the managers who were most effective at harnessing deadlines. Without reading any papers in *American Economic Review*, without running a census or giving out free cake, they knew how effective short deadlines could be, and that knowledge created the space for all that followed. Likewise, by learning how to set and reset your own countdown clock, you can buy yourself whatever you most need: time to finish, time to revise, time to relax.

I want this book to be useful to anyone struggling to get work done—which is all of us. Each chapter will show you how these companies work, and will connect what you see in practice with the insights provided by behavioral scientists, psychologists, and economists. But there will also be moments when these chapters will dwell on the details of these workplaces for their own sake.

Many years ago, I read a book called *Lithography*, by Henry Cliffe. The opening lines have stuck with me, even as I've forgotten everything else in those pages: "The process of printing called lithography was invented by Aloys Senefelder about the year 1798. Tales relating to the actual discovery are many and romantic, but the facts are uncertain and need not concern us." What a disaster! I want to learn about lithography as much as the next guy, but you're skipping the romantic parts? Rest assured, that is not the way this book will proceed. When a detour into the life of an organization has proven irresistible, I have taken it.

For more than fifteen years, I've been an editor, at quarterly and monthly and weekly magazines, and I thought I knew every trick and hack and cheat to get the publication to the printer on time. But that was before I studied the workplaces you'll read about in the chapters that follow. I found ingenuity on the ground that changed the way I think about deadlines. It changed the way I wrote this book.

By assembling these deadline stories, a signal can emerge from the noise of a whole society at work. We're at a strange period in our economic lives. While I finished most of the reporting for this book before the coronavirus pandemic, I saw signs of the frailty that the crisis has uncovered in almost all of the industries I observed. The problems we're facing now have deeper roots than a single health emergency. But all of the organizations in this book had found a way to succeed despite those problems. Imagine what might happen if they could start anew, if we could take this time of transition and turn it into one of opportunity. This book aims to speak to that moment, and to the moment just about to arrive—if we can grasp it before it passes us by.

1

Creating Checkpoints: Jean-Georges Restaurants

On Monday, May 13, 2019, Jean-Georges Vongerichten got into a car outside his apartment in New York's West Village and asked to be taken to the airport. It would have been an odd time to leave town: On Tuesday he was opening a new restaurant in Lower Manhattan, on the waterfront facing Brooklyn. But Vongerichten wasn't flying anywhere. He was going to check in on another restaurant, the Paris Café, which was opening on Wednesday inside the brand-new TWA Hotel at JFK.

Opening two restaurants back to back, on consecutive days, would be impressive for Chipotle or In-N-Out Burger. It's unheard-of for a fine-dining chef like Vongerichten. It also wasn't part of the plan. The two openings had been years in the making, both tied up in larger redevelopment projects over which the chef had no control, so he could do little but watch in horror as the deadlines converged on each other: the opening date for the waterfront restaurant, the Fulton, kept getting pushed back, while the one for the Paris Café didn't budge. As late as mid-April, Vongerichten still thought he would have a few days' buffer between them, but then that, too, disappeared.

The sixty-two-year-old Vongerichten looked grumpy, or whatever grumpy turns into when it's deployed on the face of a man whose default mode is glee. The writer Jay McInerney once described him as "George Clooney crossed with a Renaissance putto," which is hard to improve upon, even as the chef has passed middle age. Now he squirmed in his seat and kept glancing out the window.

The developers of the TWA Hotel had only turned the Paris Café kitchen over to Vongerichten the day before, which was ridiculously late. At the Fulton, the kitchen was ready six weeks before opening, and his team there had been training nonstop since then. The goal for both was to stage an opening night that felt like nothing of the sort, as if the restaurant had been up and running for months. At this point it looked as if only the Fulton would make it. "It's a massive pressure," Vongerichten said.

The Fulton and the Paris Café would become Vongerichten's thirteenth and fourteenth restaurants in New York and bring his worldwide total to thirty-eight. In July, he would add two more, both in the new Four Seasons Hotel in Philadelphia. Four restaurants in three months is a lot, but 2019 was still slower than 2017, when he opened seven, in New York, Los Angeles, Singapore, São Paulo, and London. This pace is intentional. "My dream," he told me, "would be to open a restaurant a month and then get rid of it."

Even Vongerichten's detractors, those who think the individual restaurants suffer for the good of the whole, have trouble hiding their wonder at the juggernaut he has assembled. One critic, in a review of a relatively early addition to the Jean-Georges culinary universe, asked if the chef had perhaps been cloned. Vongerichten himself credits it all to "the formula," a set of procedures that he and his team put in place to make all these openings run as smoothly as possible.

In the car's backseat, Daniel Del Vecchio, executive vice president of Jean-Georges Management, was taking calls and typing away on a laptop, his hair slicked back and his eyes a little puffy. In addition to Del Vecchio, who rarely leaves Vongerichten's side, the two people who are indispensable for openings are Gregory Brainin, who leads a sort of commando unit that trains cooks at Jean-Georges restaurants all over the world, and Lois Freedman, the president of the company and the only person I saw overrule Vongerichten himself. All of them had been with the company for decades. "We're a very tight-knit group," Del Vecchio said. When they started, they were simply cooks, but they grew into executives as the business grew. They now oversee 5,000 employees in twelve countries. (Facebook, by comparison had only 3,200 employees when it went public.) Last year, the Jean-Georges group earned $350 million in total sales.

In the car, Vongerichten took a call from the fish supplier for his New York restaurants, running through a list of sea creatures that grew increasingly obscure as he went down it. He and Del Vecchio then talked about the new menus they were having printed for Jean-Georges, the chef's flagship restaurant on Central Park. They had decided to scrap the à la carte menu and offer only a six- or ten-course tasting, each in both omnivore and vegetarian versions. Vongerichten called it a "major change," the biggest move he has made since Jean-Georges opened in 1997.

The menu change wasn't just innovation for its own sake. They had an audience in mind. In 2018, the reviewers for the *Michelin Guide* downgraded the restaurant from three stars to two—the first time Jean-Georges hadn't earned the top ranking since Michelin started covering New York. "That was a sad day for us," Freedman told me. "I was sad for him because he is a chef who's always in his restaurants. Even though he's really busy, he's always in his restaurants working."

Hidden in that defense is a problem that has been haunting Vongerichten and his team. Is it even possible to run a three-star restaurant and a globe-spanning corporation at the same time? The first is meant to offer a once-in-a-lifetime experience, while the second depends on being able to take that experience and repackage it for different audiences, cuisines, and budgets. To find someone able to do both is incredibly rare, as if Leonardo da Vinci were able to produce both *The Last Supper* and *Last Supper* tote bags. Most of Vongerichten's peers don't even try: The median number of restaurants for a three-Michelin-star chef in the United States is two.

If Vongerichten didn't love both equally—the empire and its namesake—his choice would be easy. Only the spinoffs earn him any money. He's also proud of the system he's built to open restaurants all over the globe. "We have it down to a science with our team, with Lois and Greg and Danny and everybody," he says. "We know how to put it all together." But Vongerichten started his career in France, as a teenage apprentice in a Michelin three-star kitchen, and that rarefied world maintains an unshakable grip on his imagination.

His team is no less committed. Brainin got angry just thinking about the lost star. "We fight like hell every day to ensure that the consistency, the power of the dishes, the pristinity of the ingredients is spot-on every single time without flaws," he said. (*Pristinity*, one assumes, combines pristineness and divinity, which is an accurate reflection of Brainin's attitude toward food.) They had already contacted Michelin and asked them to hold off making their determination for this year's guide until they had tried the new menu.

So that was the goal for the week: open two restaurants, keep the other thirty-eight running, and somehow start to convince an anonymous group of judges from a tire company that Jean-Georges remains one of the best dining experiences in the world. For the first time since we left the West Village, Vongerichten grew silent. But then he saw the sign for the TWA Hotel and he yelped with happiness. "Look," he said, "there's our staff!" Pressed up against the second-floor window of the restaurant was a group of about forty servers and line cooks. They would be using the kitchen for the first time that day. The first customers would be arriving in forty-eight hours.

To get a sense of what Vongerichten has built, and how he became a deadline savant, it might help to learn his breakfast schedule when he's in New York. He doesn't cook in his (huge, immaculate) kitchen at home but rather tours his restaurants. On Monday he eats at the Mercer, in SoHo; on Tuesday he's at the Mark, on the Upper East Side; on Wednesday he's at ABCV, in the Flatiron District; Thursday is the wild card; and Friday it's breakfast at Jean-Georges.

His restaurants don't feel as if they are part of a chain—though in a manner of speaking, they are. They aren't hotel restaurants, though a small number of them are in hotels. And, with the exception of Jean-Georges, they aren't formal dining rooms, though the service at each exudes some of the stateliness of the highest-end, black-tie-and-silver-cloche places. They resemble instead a species of restaurant that has proliferated with the rise of the middle-class foodie. Precise but not fussy. Lush but not luxe. Expensive but not meant for expense accounts. A place you might go on a date night.

Most of the restaurants in this class are one-offs, neighborhood joints created by culinary-school grads and sous chefs who have reached escape velocity from whatever kitchens they trained in. These are passion projects—the realization of a single chef's vision now that she finally gets to run her own shop. The bewildering trick that Vongerichten and his team have pulled off is to replicate these labors of love, but at scale. The result is a group of restaurants that feels more like a commonwealth of independent states than an evil empire. A single sensibility inflects them—French technique, Asian spices, light, acidic sauces—but the joy the Jean-Georges team takes in making each place new is apparent. "That's the best part: creating a menu, a concept," Vongerichten said. "The hardest part is to keep it running for the next twenty years."

The highlight reel is impressive: potato-and-goat-cheese terrine with arugula juice at JoJo (Vongerichten, Freedman, and Del Vecchio go there for it every Tuesday); scallops with cauliflower and caper-raisin emulsion at Jean-Georges (a version of which Brainin and Vongerichten use to test new chefs during the hiring process); tuna and tapioca pearls with Thai chiles, Sichuan peppercorns, cinnamon, chipotle, and makrut lime at Spice Market ("We've never made food that complicated again," Brainin said); wild-mushroom burdock noodles, tempeh, and pickles at ABCV (reflecting Vongerichten's recent preoccupation with health and environmental sustainability). The molten-chocolate cake that took over dessert menus all over the country in the aughts? That came from the menu at Lafayette, the first New York restaurant run by Vongerichten, which he left in 1991.

It's astounding how consistently his system works. It's one thing to build something that looks like a neighborhood gem. It's another to make it a place that people want to go, producing dishes that sway even critics who might otherwise grumble about the whole towering Jean-Georges edifice. (Pete Wells recently coined the term *Vongerichtenstein* in a review for the *New York Times*.) Each new restaurant is instantly a Best New Restaurant.

We are suspicious of such profligacy. The metaphors shift from the realm of art to those of the business world: Vongerichten has built a factory, a franchise, an assembly line. You might imagine an enterprise of cut-and-paste, from the lighting in the dining room to the items on the menu. The reality, however, is weirder, a space where rigidity and a more freewheeling spirit can mix.

———

The Fulton was born five years ago, in a boardroom overlooking New York Harbor. Its parents were Jean-Georges Management and the Howard Hughes Corporation, the century-old oil, real estate, and aircraft company that has been redeveloping Manhattan's South Street Seaport. Howard Hughes asked Vongerichten to install a restaurant inside Pier 17, a boxy mall on stilts that they were building over the East River. Vongerichten had always wanted to open a seafood restaurant, and here was a space that couldn't be any closer to the water, steps from the former Fulton Fish Market. The location determined the concept and the name.

And, for a while, that's all he had. Construction dragged on, and Vongerichten refuses to begin planning a menu until a restaurant's design is locked in. Freedman takes the lead during this phase, choosing everything from the color of the banquettes (sea-foam green) to the price point of the water glasses (Pure by Pascale Naessens for Serax—a name only Douglas Adams could love, and just over $7 each wholesale).

Freedman started working for Vongerichten at Lafayette, right out of cooking school. Then, in 1991, together with investor Phil Suarez, they opened a bistro called JoJo. Freedman took over the business end of the restaurant and soon found out she had a knack for it. "I wanted to be able to grow my fingernails and dress up," she said. "In the kitchen, both of my arms all the way up had burn marks." When she started, did she imagine she would eventually be running thirty-eight restaurants? "I didn't think past JoJo at the time," she said. "No one had multiple restaurants. That just wasn't what people did back then. Chefs were not expanding."

At the Fulton, menu planning began in January, once construction was far enough along that Vongerichten and Brainin felt comfortable hiring an executive chef, who would run the restaurant day to day. Normally the Jean-Georges team would promote a sous chef from the flagship to lead the new venture, like a plant propagated through cuttings. But this time they plucked a young chef named Noah Poses from the Watergate Hotel, after a trial tasting that impressed Brainin enough that he didn't even make Poses audition for Vongerichten himself.

Poses, Brainin, and Vongerichten spent about three months experimenting in the Jean-Georges kitchen until they had a rough draft of a menu. In March, they moved to the kitchen at the Fulton. There they continued to refine the dishes, cutting some and adding others. Anchovies were on the menu (environmentally friendly), and then they were off (not enough people like them). They added snow crab to the risotto. ("Once Jean-Georges tries a better version of something," Brainin said, "there's no selling him on going back.") Some dishes were judged too hard to make in a reasonable amount of time, but a labor-intensive Manhattan clam chowder was included at the last minute because it's just too popular to ignore.

Newly hired servers learn everything from how to clear a plate from a table to how to talk about the sourcing of the fish. "I don't mind the knife to be a little crooked on the table, but the person must have a personality, and they must be able to sell," Vongerichten said. Freedman told me she likes hiring actors as servers because they can memorize long blocks of text.

Once Poses brought his four sous chefs on board in April, they could begin the most important part of the opening process:

simulating a real dinner service as early and often as possible. The first of these daily mock services was offered to just twenty employees, then thirty, then forty—until eventually the team opening the Fulton would pull staff members from the corporate office, from the Howard Hughes Corporation, and from their vendors to fill the restaurant. These daily checkpoints on the way to the final deadline were a big part of what Vongerichten meant by his "formula." They were the secret to flawless openings and satisfied customers.

At the end of each day, Brainin, Vongerichten, and Poses would take the menu they had planned and tweak it, dish by dish. Or, more precisely, gram by gram: Everything in a Jean-Georges restaurant is measured to the gram, and deviations are not allowed. "We make sure that we test, we test, we test, and test again," Vongerichten said.

At the final mock service, one week before opening, a line cook prepared a kale salad. Brainin quizzed him on the number of grams of olive oil, of kale leaves, of Parmesan in the salad, and the cook rattled off each one by heart. The cook placed the partly assembled salad on a scale and shaved Parmesan onto it until he hit the desired number. It was ready to serve.

Later, after eating an entire bowl of tagliatelle with clams, Brainin announced that it needed six more grams of olive oil—a little more than a teaspoon—and then it would be done. Compare this with Bill Buford's description of the same dish in *Heat*, his account of working in Mario Batali's kitchen: "the only ingredient that's measured is the pasta. . . . Everything else is what you pick with your fingertips, and it's either a small pinch or a large pinch or something in between: not helpful, but that, alas, is the way quantities are determined in a restaurant."

I asked one of the culinary trainers working under Brainin

if the cooks ever objected to the rigidness of all this gram-counting. "It sounds tedious," he said, "but you learn to respect the ingredients and the dish." Obeying the scales was like obeying the rules of a sonnet—a limitation that allowed for almost unlimited artistry. Vongerichten said it was also a clear-cut way to ensure that, even if he weren't cooking in all thirty-eight of his kitchens, the dishes would still be true to his vision, without any unhelpful improvisations by local cooks. The only other way to achieve the same end would be to radically downsize: "I would have a counter with seven seats. I cook, I serve you, and I clean. That would be J.G. one hundred percent."

Shortly before the first mock diners arrived, Vongerichten walked through the restaurant. The paper that had covered the windows during construction had just been torn down, so he could see the main selling point, visually, of the location: a full-span view of the Brooklyn Bridge along one whole wall of the restaurant. Vongerichten pronounced it "spectacular." There were long suede banquettes, nautical-themed lighting that tiptoed right up to Long John Silver territory (lots of hemp), and a hand-painted mural with a Jules Verne vibe on the wall. The chef made his way through the kitchen, the dishwashing area, the patio, the balcony, even the bathrooms. It felt a bit like a Wes Anderson sequence, with various attendants coming up to him with quick yes-or-no queries. The men hanging the sign above the main entrance asked for his okay and he nodded.

Mock service itself resembles normal service, with a few important differences. The guests receive menus, but with their choices highlighted for them. Otherwise, Brainin said, everyone would order the lobster and the kitchen wouldn't be tested properly. Each guest got one signature cocktail, one appetizer, and one entree. Brainin held up the menu of someone who would be compelled to order the Shiso Gin and Tonic, the Crispy Soft Shell Crabs, and the Parmesan Cheese and Lemon Risotto.

As the orders started to come in, Poses took his position by the pass-through to the kitchen. Brainin was on the line, but he would come out frequently to frown over a plate of food with his new hire. Poses, who was thirty-two, had a young face, and when he and Brainin conferred, it had the appearance of a manager's visit to the mound to talk it out with a rookie fast-baller. One problem became apparent right away: the runners kept getting backed up near the pass-through to the kitchen. To explain why, Brainin pulled me over to the window to read a ticket. It was a long list of orders for a single table, some hot, some cold, some quick to prepare, and some requiring a nonnegotiably long cook time. The best kitchens will figure out how to prepare everything to come together at the right moment. This kitchen hadn't gotten there yet, so runners waited with half-full trays for the last item to be finished so they could serve everything at once.

"Your first month," Poses told me, "no one knows what they're doing, at all, which is expected. From the cook to the dishwasher, to the runner to the server to even myself. You go in with a plan, knowing that that plan won't really work." The runner problem was the kind of issue that only became apparent when they had enough orders to throw off their timing. They'd have to figure out a way to fix it.

Poses and Brainin both seemed happy with the food. Or Poses did, and Brainin seemed to alternate between intense confidence and a neurotic insistence that the dishes were *almost* perfect, if he could just find that final knob to tune. The standard he aimed for, he said, was addictively delicious: "Meaning, even if you're not hungry anymore you're compelled to take another bite."

Brainin had been working for David Burke, at the Park

Avenue Café, when Vongerichten's first book, *Simple Cuisine*, came out in 1990. "Every time we got a break, the cooks and I would go hover over that book," he said. From *Simple Cuisine*, he hit upon the central metaphor that still animates his cooking: the three-note chord. Every dish should have three main flavors that together produce something greater than themselves. He went to work for Vongerichten a few years later. Brainin thinks he caught Vongerichten's eye because he was the cleanest cook in the kitchen. That was something he had learned from David Burke, who once gave a kitchen tour to a group of customers and stopped to watch Brainin work: "He announced to everybody to look at my station and what a disgusting shithole it was." Was he right? "One hundred percent right. And I've been the cleanest cook in any kitchen I've ever worked since."

As the mock service ended, Freedman was texting with Vongerichten about the butter that came with the bread. At the moment it was a little squirt of butter mixed with crème fraiche. Freedman wanted something simpler: "Nice, beautiful, salted butter. You can slice it." By the following week, the butter had changed.

Downstairs, the line cooks were wiping down the kitchen. Brainin and Vongerichten were talking through the decision to put fluke crudo on the menu. A few months earlier, *New York* had published an article with the headline "Fluke Crudo Is a Scourge That Must Be Stopped," but the chefs decided they couldn't give up something that was local, sustainable, and versatile just because some critic wanted to plant a flag in the ground. Plus, "we love that fish." To fend off any complaints of unoriginality, they had added a fermented habanero vinaigrette to it, along with something called Sichuan bud.

During the service, Brainin noted, one line cook "completely fucked up" the sauce that comes with the burger, making it twice as salty as it was supposed to be. He asked her to prep the burger again while he watched. She cooked it all the way again and made the same mistake. Only when he was there step by step, from prep to finished product, did he spot the problem. Now imagine the same process, repeated for every dish and every line cook. "No other kitchen runs this way," Brainin said, "even if they say they do." It's also why you can be assured of a good Jean-Georges meal whether you're in New York or Jakarta or Guangzhou.

It was six o'clock. All the guests had left, after turning in a mock service questionnaire asking, among other subjects, whether they had been greeted with a smile, whether a server came to the table within sixty seconds of their being seated, and how each of the dishes might be improved. I asked Poses what came next. He said that there are some problems they would address in the end-of-mock meeting, most important the runners backing up near the kitchen. But other kinks in the system wouldn't even be visible until they had a full dining room and paying customers. Brainin compared it to learning to ride a bike on a short driveway. You can do it a thousand times, but you won't really be tested until you hit the road, you hit a pothole, and you get doored.

The mock services are the most important part of the Jean-Georges formula for two reasons: first, these checkpoints guarantee steady progress toward opening day—each one is a miniature rehearsal of the deadline effect. Second, they are a way to ensure that, when that day arrives, the restaurant will be as close to perfect as possible. To understand why these meals, interim deadlines on the way to the final deadline, are so effective, let's leave the restaurant world behind for a moment.

Two decades ago, the behavioral economist Dan Ariely, together with his colleague Klaus Wertenbroch, conducted an experiment that demonstrates the power of interim deadlines. Ariely was teaching at MIT at the time, and he told the students in his consumer behavior class that they would have three papers due before the end of the twelve-week semester. All the papers would be graded after the last day of class, but the students could submit them at any time before then. The twist: they had to commit to a deadline for each of the three papers. "The dates were binding," Ariely and Wertenbroch wrote, "such that each day of delay beyond the deadline would cause a 1 percent penalty in the paper's overall grade."

The rational approach would be to make the last day of class the deadline for all three papers: that would remove the possibility of a penalty and give the students the most time and flexibility to research and write. Some of the students did just that and submitted all three papers on the last day of class. But others knew themselves better than that. They set early deadlines for the first two papers, and by doing so forced themselves to start working on the projects earlier in the semester.

To complete the experiment, Ariely set different rules for two other classes. They had the same three papers to write, but one class was told to turn in all their work at the end of the semester. The last class was given a mandatory deadline for each paper, spaced evenly at four weeks, eight weeks, and twelve weeks.

Once all the papers were in and graded, Ariely compared the results. The students with mandatory, evenly spaced deadlines did the best, and the students who had to turn in all their papers on the last day of class did the worst. The most interesting result, though, came from the class that chose its own deadlines. As a group, they did worse than the class with mandatory due dates. But that effect disappeared when Ariely excluded the scores of those who had chosen to submit their papers on the last day of the semester. "The students who did not space their deadlines sufficiently pulled the average grades of this class down," Ariely wrote. Whether self-imposed or mandatory, interim deadlines were the most effective means of getting a higher grade.

Once the mock services at the Fulton started, they became a daily interim deadline, an opportunity for the staff to test their skills and consolidate their knowledge. They also became progressively harder, as Vongerichten ratcheted up the number of diners from twenty to forty. The progress made each day had the side effect of keeping the servers and cooks motivated. In an article for the *Harvard Business Review*, the researchers Teresa Amabile and Steven J. Kramer wrote about the psychological effect of what they called "small wins" for teams working on a project.

"When we think about progress, we often imagine how good it feels to achieve a long-term goal or experience a major breakthrough," they wrote. "These big wins are great—but they are relatively rare. The good news is that even small wins can boost inner work life tremendously." They asked members of a team working at a tech company to respond to a daily survey of how they felt about their jobs. One of the most positive days for one programmer came not at the end of a big project, but right in the middle: "I figured out why something was not working correctly. I felt relieved and happy because this was a minor milestone for me."

Brainin, Poses, and the sous chefs at the Fulton celebrated each successful mock service with language more peppery than that, but the underlying sentiment was the same. When building something with as many moving parts as a brand-new restaurant, each small step along the way feels like a victory.

By some measures, that there are only dozens of Jean-Georges restaurants is evidence of restraint. Almost daily, the team is asked about opening up a new restaurant somewhere in the world. They say yes only to the most extraordinary offers.

Unfortunately for anyone at Jean-Georges Management

hoping for a quieter year, the TWA Hotel, which had taken for its lobby Eero Saarinen's 1962 TWA terminal, a neo-futurist landmark recognized as a masterpiece from the day of its completion, was judged too good an opportunity to pass up. It had been a three-year project, but from the hotel's appearance two days before opening, it might have been better if the developers had given themselves a few more weeks. When Vongerichten showed up that day, workers were hammering, drilling, and sawing. The entrance to the restaurant was nearly blocked off with boxes and wire racks: Riedel glasses, latex gloves, ketchup. Wires hung from the ceiling. The cooks weren't allowed in the kitchen yet, so they sat bored in the dining room, sprawled out on the white Saarinen tulip chairs. The wait staff was crowding another section, about forty of them going through their first orientation. There was a big box of Dunkin' Donuts coffee on the counter. Vongerichten tried a sip and grimaced. Someone ran off to make him an espresso.

Everyone was saying a variation of the same thing: it was insane that they were trying to open in two days. I saw Freedman sitting near one of Saarinen's soaring glass windows, looking cold and perturbed. One of the glass panels was missing. A sheet of plastic flapped in its place. I asked Freedman if she thought they'd be able to open the restaurant in time. "Not really," she said.

Freedman said the big problem right now was that she couldn't envision the finished product. How would she know they were using the wrong kind of butter if they didn't even have plates? There were hints, though, of what it would look like once they cleared the junk away. It was a fantasia from the atomic age: There were Knoll tables, standing lamps that looked like armillary spheres, and white banquettes that echoed the swoop of Saarinen's roof. Lois was squinting at it all. "The tulip chairs," she said. "They swivel, and I thought they were going to be stationary." If they swiveled, the servers would have to spend all their time realigning them. Or worse, they wouldn't.

Noon passed and the kitchen still wasn't ready. The open window made the room cold enough that a few of the cooks huddled around the pizza oven for warmth.

It might be worth pausing here to explain how Vongerichten and his team found themselves in this position. There are two types of restaurants that carry the Jean-Georges name: the ones they own and the ones they only operate. Vongerichten and his partners own Jean-Georges, JoJo, and Perry Street. Most of the others, and all the restaurants outside of New York, are management deals, which constitute three-quarters of Vongerichten's total business. For about 6 percent of gross revenue and 10 percent of net, Jean-Georges Management designs the restaurant and runs the kitchen, but a partner owns or leases the space, does payroll, pays vendors, and, ultimately, takes home any profits after the licensing fees are paid. (In the event of a disaster like the coronavirus pandemic, the partner also absorbs all of the losses. That left Vongerichten better positioned than some restaurateurs to make a comeback after the crisis.)

The problem with the management deals is that the owner sets the schedule. And they can respond to construction delays, which hit both the Fulton and the Paris Café, in one of two ways: they can also delay the restaurant opening until everything is ready, or they can decide to move ahead regardless. The developers for the TWA Hotel had set a ribbon-cutting for Wednesday and invited the press and Governor Andrew Cuomo. There would be no more delays.

By early afternoon, the kitchen was still not ready. Vongerichten and his team had tried their best to adapt to the circumstances. Most important, they had sent Amy Sur-Trevino, the executive chef, and her sous chefs on a tour of the Jean-Georges kitchens of New York to fine-tune their technique.

But even Del Vecchio, who usually mirrors Vongerichten's enthusiasm, looked troubled. "To be honest with you, it's very stressful," he says. "We should be finishing training and we're just getting started."

The servers at least were getting their briefing, though they had to leave the dining room, which was still being set up, to get it. Over the echo of a reciprocating saw, I could hear a trainer instruct them in the proper pronunciation of menu items like *crémant de Bourgogne*. Nearby, a group of dancers was rehearsing a flash-mob-style number they would perform at the ribbon cutting, now just forty hours away.

In the history of the Jean-Georges empire, there are two eras: before Spice Market and after Spice Market. That restaurant, which opened in Manhattan's Meatpacking District in 2004, was the beginning of an era of rapid expansion for the company. It was also the venue for which Brainin and the others created the detailed prep system they now use everywhere. They had to: the dishes, which drew freely from Indian and Southeast Asian cuisines, had long lists of ingredients that had to be precisely calibrated.

To plan the menu, Vongerichten took Brainin, Del Vecchio, and a few others on an eighteen-day research trip to India, Malaysia, Thailand, Vietnam, and Indonesia. The rule was that everyone could bring only carry-on luggage. Del Vecchio kept a journal of that time, and reading it is a window into travel the Jean-Georges way. There are a lot of passages like "We arrived to a local band and elephants. We went to the palace and met Princess Bhargavi and Maharana Arvind Singhji Mewar for cocktails" and "We all went for massages at the Oriental, great as usual, then to dinner." There are also lists after lists of ingredients, spices and sauces and herbs, that had rarely been seen in the New York fine-dining scene before, until Vongerichten put them on his menu. After it opened, and until Vongerichten sold it in 2008, the restaurant was almost always packed, serving as many as a thousand covers a night. (In 2019, the most profitable Jean-Georges restaurant was Prime at the Bellagio in Las Vegas. It and Jean-Georges both had revenues of $25 million a year, but all of the flagship's profits disappear in food and staffing costs.)

Once the team had proved itself up to the logistical challenge of Spice Market, everything seemed within reach: a spinoff in São Paulo, a steakhouse in Vegas, a pizza place in Shanghai. Openings became carefully choreographed deployments of the team of culinary trainers and mock services. Regular operations ran smoothly because of the gram-by-gram approach, together with weekly phone calls from Del Vecchio. Licensing deals helped address all the messy business of construction and permitting and payroll.

The Fulton made use of all the resources the company had developed in its rapid expansion. Before the first paying customers would arrive, though, there was one more test: two friends-and-family dinners. These meals, which are common in the restaurant world, were as close as the Fulton would get to a regular night of service before the actual opening. Unlike the mock services, the guests could pick what they wanted from the menu. They could even, like paying customers, make special requests and send dishes back and otherwise be pains in the ass.

The menu had a warning up top: "Thank you for helping us during Family and Friends! We ask that you order one appetizer, one entree, and one dessert per person." Vongerichten wandered around, on and off his phone. I asked him if he felt ready and he said, "Yes, it's time. We had plenty of training." He seemed a little nervous.

I noticed one of the tables wobbling. I had always wondered

when that particular affliction sets in, and now I know that it can start on day one. Or day negative four. Other than that, the restaurant looked calm and buttoned-up. I knew the menu, though, so I could see some evidence of last-minute strain, a peek under the water that proved that duck madly paddling. The risotto was off the menu, as was the kampachi and the sea bass for two. I'd later learn reasons for all three: they couldn't find affordable snow crab for the risotto. The kampachi wouldn't be popular enough on a relatively quiet night to sell out, and they had a dark weekend coming up, which would mean letting it spoil. And the sea bass was available, just off menu. They had prepared eight of them for special guests, or what they called PXes (*personnes extraordinaires*).

With 105 covers, the most they'd done yet, Poses said they would learn which parts of the menu create bottlenecks: "The dish might be great, but is it feasible for a cook to turn out a hundred of them?" Because people could choose their courses, Poses said, they would also have some of their first feedback on what will be popular: "It's cool to have a lot of different items on the menu, but what do people want? What will make them happy?"

Poses said this with a democratic forthrightness, but the question was more fraught than he was letting on. Like any artform, cooking makes competing demands on its practitioners. Would a chef try to please the market, the critics, or himself? A lot of the fuss over bad reviews and stars awarded or taken away reflected the extent to which critics had created a separate ecosystem of culinary value. In that world, fluke crudo was a cliché. Critics want novelty and will punish a restaurant for not giving it to them.

Most chefs' tastes probably hew closer to the critics', but they also have to make a living. Brainin made this point by talking about tuna tartare. Tuna tartare, he said, is the most popular appetizer everywhere in the country. At a seafood restaurant like the Fulton, they couldn't leave it off the menu. So it's on there. There are edgier dishes right next to it, ones that Brainin and Poses and Vongerichten are more excited about, but by even having it as an option, they risk that a reviewer would come and sniff about the lack of originality, the same old tired tartare found on every menu in the city. They tried to get around this problem by experimenting at the margins: keep soy sauce off the plate and replace it with a yuzu mustard sauce and crispy shaved fennel. (The three-note chord: the fresh fish, the mustard, the licorice of the fennel. Also Pink Lady apple puree and tarragon powder. Maybe it's more of a diminished seventh chord.) The risk, and the reward, of giving people what they already want is that you become the Jeff Koons of the culinary world. Beloved by all, esteemed by no one.

So Vongerichten and Brainin and Poses were in an uneasy place. Trying to innovate for the critics without alienating their audience. And not to get too deep in the Aristotle 101 weeds here, but what ultimately constitutes a good life, for a chef or for anyone? Is it to make uncompromising art, or to make people happy? What if the purest expression of your art *is* making people happy?

The people at the friends-and-family dinner voted, in any case, and they chose lobster. They served sixty-five of them that night. But if there was one dish that Brainin and Poses and Vongerichten were most excited about, something meant to be both a showstopper and comfortingly familiar, it was the sea bass en croute: a whole sea bass for two, head on, served underneath a flaky crust. "It's the one," Vongerichten said. "It's a classic that nobody else is doing in town." He called it a fourth-generation dish: Fernand Point, author of *Ma Gastronomie,* developed it at La Pyramide in France, passed it on to Louis Outhier, who taught it to Vongerichten at L'Oasis near Cannes, who taught it to Poses.

The sous chefs put one up on the pass-through, and Vongerichten and Freedman followed it upstairs to a table of four. The pastry had been etched with the tip of a paring knife and painted in egg wash to give it fishy definition: scales, eyes, spines in the fins. The crust was cut tableside with scissors and placed on the edge of the platter. The skin was peeled back, and the fillets were moved to a plate, deboned, reunited with the pastry, and served with some tomatoes and hollandaise. The whole ceremony felt both formal and whimsical. "It's beyond," Freedman said.

By nine o'clock, the downstairs had mostly emptied, but the upstairs had become almost rowdy. Freedman wasn't eating yet: Del Vecchio and Vongerichten would probably sit down with her around eleven. In the meantime, Del Vecchio claimed a place at the bar, where he was trying to solve a seating problem at one of the restaurants uptown via a WhatsApp chat with the staff there. As he typed, he got a text from Singapore congratulating everyone back in New York on the impending opening of the Fulton.

At the ribbon-cutting ceremony, the Paris Café looked almost finished, save for a few stray wires hanging from the ceiling. They hadn't been able to conduct any mock services, and there wouldn't be a friends-and-family meal. But Sur-Trevino's kitchen was putting up plates, even if there was no one to serve or eat them. By 10:00 a.m., there were five poached eggs lined up, untouched, on the pass-through.

Freedman and Del Vecchio reminisced about past crunch times, trying to decide if this was the most crazed they'd ever been. Del Vecchio said he knows he's busy when he gets up to take a shower and the towel is still wet from the night before.

Vongerichten arrived and shook everyone's hands, a bit

stiltedly. One young employee said it was the first time she'd ever shaken his hand. "Well," he said, "I've never opened two restaurants at the same time before."

The ribbon-cutting ceremony in the lobby was delayed — Cuomo — and the crowd was growing restless. Someone had brought in pastries from the French bakery Ladurée, which Freedman was using to dress up the otherwise empty steel counters of the kitchen. (A Potemkin restaurant, for now.) Vongerichten, however, couldn't let an opportunity to feed and delight people pass him by, so it became a race between him and Freedman to see if she could put a pastry on a display platter before he took it out into the lobby to give away.

At first no one noticed that it was Vongerichten himself serving croissants. Several people grabbed one without looking up. But when someone recognized him, there was a rush to get a snack and a selfie with the chef. Within minutes, he had given everything away and posed for dozens of pictures.

Earlier, Vongerichten told me about the day Michelin took the third star away. "We were shocked," he said, not least because nothing had changed from the year before: "We couldn't understand because it's the same chef, same team." Unlike Brainin, though, who thought the whole system was bizarre and inconsistent ("It's hard to pin the tail on the donkey," he said, "if you can't see the donkey"), Vongerichten took the message Michelin was sending to heart. After the news was out, he wrote to them to ask for them to tell him all the weaknesses they saw. Some of the sauces were too runny. The shared space with Nougatine, Jean-Georges's sister restaurant, was confusing. All minor matters, Vongerichten said, but the critiques were right. To be a three-star, there was no room for an off night.

Regaining his lost Michelin star, Vongerichten decided, would require a sacrifice of sorts. Jean-Georges is famous for its regulars, the loyal customers who come week after week and order the same thing from the lengthy à la carte menu. These are not people looking for a multi-course vegetarian tasting. But Vongerichten had noticed a shift years earlier: "When you go to a high-end restaurant now, from Eleven Madison to Masa to Brooklyn Fare"—three of the five restaurants in New York that have the highest Michelin rating—"you have like, ten courses, they bring you to the kitchen for a drink, they have a whole experience, a greater experience than going to Restaurant Daniel and having three courses." (Daniel dropped from three stars to two in the 2015 guide.)

Vongerichten had resisted making the same move for years, but he could avoid it no longer. The new standard had come to resemble the old standard, from the days when Michelin was intended for people on road trips, and the three-star restaurant was defined explicitly as a place worth "a special journey." The loss of the star moved Vongerichten to feel it was time to "claim our status again. I mean at least try, give it a shot. Because I think our food is there. It's very special."

Shortly after the ribbon-cutting at the Paris Café, Freedman told me a story from the beginning of her time with Vongerichten, right after the *New York Times* published a four-star review of Lafayette, an event that changed both their lives. A customer sat down and, seemingly unaware of the greatness of the dining room he'd found himself in, ordered scrambled eggs. Scrambled eggs, that's it. Vongerichten made them himself—"He made the best scrambled eggs of his life"—and then topped it with caviar, crème fraiche, and chives. "That taught me so much as a young chef," Freeman said. "It wasn't about ego. It was about what the customer wanted to eat."

Freedman had felt rushed and dissatisfied, she said, throughout the run-up to the Paris Café opening. The crucial missing link were the mock services: without the normal run of daily deadlines to fine-tune the food, the service, and presentation, the normal polish associated with a Jean-Georges restaurant never materialized. The staff there were like Ariely's students who had to finish all their papers at the end of the semester—there was no way they would get the same high grade as the clockwork operation over at the Fulton.

Still, it was easy to imagine how much more dire it would have been if Freedman and her team weren't running it. Sur-Trevino and her cooks would have had nowhere to practice before this weekend. There wouldn't be a team of culinary trainers there to assist them. The makeup of the dishes would have wobbled all over the place, rather than obeying the list and the scale. The chairs would have swiveled out of position. Instead, on opening night, the Paris Café was probably the worst of Vongerichten's thirty-eight restaurants, but it was also one of the better restaurants in the city.

The first paying customers in the history of the Fulton arrived at 5:30. Multiple hostesses greeted them, took their coats, and showed them to their seats. They weren't friends or family or PXes. They had made their reservation using an app.

Poses gave a start-of-service speech to his staff, stressing the importance of moving tickets along quickly to the runners, and then the first orders started to come in. "It's a whole new set of challenges," he told me. I asked if he was nervous. "I go into every service with a certain level of anxiety," he said, "but I don't think it's necessarily an unhealthy amount of anxiety. It's a normal chef feeling, the anxiety."

Vongerichten is known as an easygoing boss, and Poses seemed to be made in that mold. He had been cooking since he was a child, the son of a restaurant owner and chef in Philadelphia, and he had made his way up via the Modern in Manhattan. It's a big deal to open a restaurant, he said. You are creating its reputation from scratch, rather than inheriting whatever came before you, both good and bad.

Poses had opened a restaurant before, the Mildred in Philadelphia. He started as a cook there, in 2012, and was eventually promoted to chef de cuisine. The restaurant didn't last: business was inconsistent, the staff didn't always work together the way they should. "Maybe part of that was due to not setting up those systems and training staff properly," Poses said. The experience had made him a big believer in the Jean-Georges way of opening a restaurant. "Look at this room," he said. "Look at the support. If I were doing this by myself, I would probably have no hair and would be shaking."

At that moment, Vongerichten arrived. "It feels good in here," he said. He noticed a young woman eating alone at the bar, and wondered if it was perhaps Hannah Goldfield, the food critic from *The New Yorker*. It was not, and I told him so, but he didn't believe me. He ran over to the pass-through and grabbed a printout with headshots of prominent restaurant critics, including Goldfield, Pete Wells of the *Times*, and Adam Platt of *New York*. He showed it to me and pointed to Goldfield, then looked again at the woman at the bar. Okay, he admitted, false alarm.

We watched as Brainin demonstrated proper plating of the kampachi, with mounds of radish sitting atop the fish, to one cook. Freedman was at the hostess stand, solving a seating problem. Five men who lived in the neighborhood wanted a table but didn't have a reservation. They handed Freedman $100 (for the staff, they said), and she said she would see what she could do. After a minute, during which she added the money to the staff tip pool, she told the men she could seat them. They were ecstatic.

In certain moods, Vongerichten will talk wistfully about the simpler days of having just one restaurant to run, when all he had to worry about was Lafayette or JoJo. Downsizing, if he could ever do it, could also provide the quickest path back to that third Michelin star: Critics want ceaseless innovation from a chef, but they also reward something closer to asceticism. The solitary genius, presiding over the counter with seven seats. It's a more appealing story than the chef who can open seven restaurants in a year.

Vongerichten's dilemma is that the drive that made Lafayette and Jean-Georges great is the same one that made it impossible to stop with just one or two restaurants. It's the desire to say yes to everything, to solve every problem, to make everybody happy. "I went into this business," he said, "because I love to pamper and tend to people." If you had the ability to do that in eighteen cities on four continents, rather than in one restaurant on Central Park, wouldn't you?

It was dark now, and the lights shining on the Brooklyn Bridge reflected off the water. Brainin stepped back and admired the line at work. It never ceased to amaze him, he said, watching a kitchen come together. Three weeks ago, they could barely serve twenty meals without panicking. Now they were doing 140. "Opening a restaurant is like having a baby," he said. "It's a strenuous, arduous, complicated process. You've got to be sure that the baby can breathe on its own and eat on its own and walk on its own and grow on its own." He would keep coming to the Fulton every night for a month. "After that I will be here at least once a week, you know, forever."

He turned back to the kitchen, where Poses and Vongerichten were conferring over a dish. If it wasn't already perfect, it was a gram or two away at most.

2

Planning Right to Left: Easter Lilies and Airbus Jets

If you take the Redwood Highway down from Oregon, cross the border into California, and drive up over the Klamath Mountains until you run out of road, you'll wind up on a little plateau overlooking the Pacific Ocean. It's a place that never gets too hot in the summer, never gets too cold in the winter, and has enough annual rainfall to make it the perfect environment to grow one rare crop: *lilium longiflorum*, the Easter lily.

There, on about three square miles of flat, arable land near the town of Smith River, are the four family farms that produce all the Easter lilies sold in the United States and Canada: ten million bulbs, give or take, depending on the year. A few decades ago, before farmers discovered that removing the buds from the plants made the bulbs bigger by harvest time, the fields would be full of the delicate white flowers every July, and people would drive from up and down the coast just to get a peek. "There's really nothing more majestic than seven, eight, ten acres of Easter lilies, all in bloom on a night of a full moon," one of the farmers told me.

You'll notice that I said the lily blooms in July, at least in this part of the world. How the growers get that flower to bloom in March or April—Easter Sunday falls on a different date every year, through a range of thirty-five days—provides us with a demonstration of deadline mastery unlike any other in the agricultural world. The team at Jean-Georges Management had used interim deadlines to make the sprint to opening day as orderly as possible. The lily farmers took that one step further: creating a plan to meet a deadline, without fail, year after year.

To see how they do it, we'll take a detour to an operation that, on its surface, couldn't look more different from the muddy fields and sheds of an Easter lily farm: the spotless assembly line of an aircraft manufacturer. We'll also learn how the farmers of Smith River avoid the trap of the planning fallacy—a quirk of human psychology that makes us chronically underestimate how much time and effort a project will require. (See also Hofstadter's Law: "It always takes longer than you expect, even when you take into account Hofstadter's Law.") The lily growers couldn't afford that error without going out of business: to miss the Easter deadline would be fatal. After all, a strawberry that ripens a week late can still be sold. When I was in Smith River, the refrain I heard was, "The day after Easter, an Easter lily is worthless."

To determine each year's schedule, the growers count back from Easter Sunday: you need at least 110 days in the greenhouse to get the plant to bloom (called forcing), after six weeks of cooling (called vernalizing) at 40°F or below—a false winter in a storage facility that happens to fall during the real North American winter. Add those days together and flip back through the calendar and you arrive somewhere between early and late October. The bulb harvest is the one variable that can move with Easter, so it does.

Linda Crockett, a second-generation lily farmer and the manager of the Del Norte County Farm Bureau, said that October is always the most hectic time on the farm. That's when what the growers do could either make or break their ability to meet the Easter deadline. Everything happens at once: laborers are pulling lily bulbs out of the ground and grading them by size; they are loading the bigger ones onto trucks and shipping them around the country; and they are replanting the smaller bulbs and bulblets for next season. Planting, harvesting, and shipping, all going on simultaneously.

When I met her one October morning, Crockett looked the part of someone in the middle of an intense, and intensely physical, deadline. She wore mud-spattered rubber boots, jeans, and a hooded sweatshirt, her short graying hair a bit mussed. "People are really tired," she told me. "I can't think of any other crop that is pushed as hard as this one."

Crockett was grumpy and bossy and solicitous all at the same time. She had a habit of cutting off a conversation by jumping in her car and driving off without explanation. In the Farm Bureau office, she saw me looking at a brochure with the title "Estimating Soil Moisture by Feel and Appearance." Photos of Trump, Pence, and secretary of agriculture Sonny Perdue stared down at us on the wall. "You won't learn anything sitting in an office," she said. She told me to join her the next day at Palmer Westbrook, where she worked part-time in the bulb-grading shed. The line started up each morning at seven.

I arrived at Palmer Westbrook, on Westbrook Lane, at six-thirty, as the first stirrings of sunrise appeared behind the mountains to the east. Smith River is a haphazard affair: a few churches, a bar, a burger joint, all on different roads, with no real center to it. The open land is a patchwork of lily fields and cow pastures, and the structures built by the four growers—usually limited to the bulb-sorting shed, a storage facility, and perhaps a greenhouse—are so small they barely register on the landscape. Yet all the Easter lilies in the country pass through those buildings.

Behind the sorting shed at Westbrook were about eight acres ready to be harvested today. Next to it, another plot had already been dug and replanted. It was 48°F, about as cold as it gets in Smith River. An eerie feeling accompanied a glance at the forecast: every day a high of 60°F, low of 45°F, with a line of suns marching down the page. Lily-growing weather. I walked around the sorting shed until I found an open door.

The building is about 200 feet long by 100 feet wide, with a high steel roof. Every day, from seven to four-thirty, the bulbs get washed, sorted, boxed, and prepared for shipping. A climate-controlled warehouse next door holds the boxes until the trucks arrive.

At the center of the sorting shed is a giant yellow apple grader, a maze of conveyor belts and chutes and scales. Easter lilies aren't a big enough industry to merit their own equipment, so all the machinery is either repurposed from a bigger corner of the ag world or fabricated in-house. They use potato diggers in the field, strawberry washers inside the shed, and apple graders to weigh and sort bulbs. The Westbrook apple grader was built by a company called FMC, which for decades also produced amphibious vehicles for the military. A plaque on the side of the machine in the Westbrook shed said Food Machinery and Chemical Corporation, which was the name the company had between 1948 and 1961.

The bulbs arrive from the field in a pallet-sized wooden box that rises to about waist high, each one holding thousands of bulbs. Those drop into a hopper, which distributes them along a moving belt, where workers remove sticks and trim out extra-long roots. Then they pass through the strawberry washers, which use sprayers to remove some of the dirt, and a shaker table filled with water, which removes the rest. The wet bulbs then drop onto the first belt of the grader, where workers place each one into an individual cup to be weighed. The machine itself automatically sorts the bulbs. The lightest ones are either replanted, sold to another farm, or composted. The bigger "commercial" ones are divided into four classes: 7/8s (for bulbs between seven and eight inches in circumference), 8/9s, 9/10s, and 10-pluses. More conveyor belts move those bulbs to the right packing station, where a worker arranges them in a box, covers them with peat moss, and sends them along the line to a storeroom before shipping. The whole operation looks like the dustiest, muddiest Rube Goldberg machine ever invented.

Before the line started up, a few men had begun assembling the wooden boxes used to ship the bulbs. These were year-round rather than seasonal employees, young men who had come to California hoping for a life of adventure. One of them, a lanky kid with a scraggly red beard, had left Pennsylvania with the hope of becoming a salmon fisherman. He spent just a few days on the water before he quit. The captain, he found out, was a drunk. "A boat is too small a place to spend with an asshole," he said. He had been with Westbrook for a year, assembling boxes, driving the forklift, doing whatever needed to be done to keep the diggers digging and the sorters sorting.

At a few minutes to seven, the line workers started to arrive. Westbrook's line was staffed entirely by women, almost all of them immigrants from Mexico and Central America. Harry

Harms, the former general manager of Hastings Inc., a grower with fields both in Smith River and across the border in Oregon, told me that was the norm. "Women are the muscle here, and every one of those muscles have to go home and cook and clean and wash for an entire family," he said. "If you can't appreciate that, you're an idiot."

About fifteen workers lined up by an electronic time-card machine to swipe in. A few hugged when they saw one another. As the seconds counted down to seven o'clock, the last of them punched the clock, and, rather quickly, they all materialized on the line. The buzzer sounded, and the belts started up. The bulbs had been left wherever they were in the process at quitting time yesterday, so everyone was immediately working full speed. By the hopper, the women grabbed errant sticks and stems that might jam in the machine. At the first station on the apple grader, they started placing the bulbs into the weighing cups. Farther down the line, they inspected the commercial bulbs to make sure the circumference matched the box for which they were bound. They wouldn't get a break until ten, then lunch, then again at two-thirty. It was exhausting work.

A few employees working the front of the belt hadn't come in today, so Crockett was trying to persuade one of the women to move. The woman was smiling at Crockett indulgently, but she seemed skeptical about following her orders. Eventually, Crockett gave up and pulled me over to the sorting line, where she grabbed a 9/10 off the belt and asked me what I saw. It looked like a denuded bulb of garlic, all fleshy cloves and no skin, with some stringy roots popping out of the bottom. No, she said, look closer. I saw that what looked like one big bulb was actually two halves that had grown together. That, Crockett said, is a double nose. If allowed to grow in a greenhouse, it would create two separate stems. A few buyers sought that out, but most wanted the standard Easter lily: one stem, a dark green nest of leaves, and five or more flared white trumpet blooms. She broke the double-nose bulb in two and threw it in the reject pile.

Crockett has been in the Easter lily business ever since the 1980s, when her father bought the lily farm across the street from their cow pasture. They named the new operation Crockett United. She was in her twenties when she started and was sixty-one now, which made her one of the most experienced people in the world at judging the commercial prospects of a bulb.

A few years ago, after her father died, Crockett had a fight with her brother over who would run the farm. Both had strong ideas about how things should be run, but her brother had a controlling share of the operation, and finally he pushed her out. They hadn't spoken since. Her brother had been surprised when she joined Westbrook, or so she had heard. "I think he thought I would go away," Crockett said, "but I don't go away."

A sort of stillness settled over the workers in the shed. Or not a stillness, since they were moving bulbs around the line as fast they could, but a steadiness, a rhythm of labor that somehow made the whole dirty, clanging, nonstop operation seem almost calm. Meeting the deadline to get the lilies shipped off in time for Easter was not a matter of achieving breakthroughs in quality and consistency like at the Fulton, or waiting for the right weather to arrive, as we'll see in the next chapter at Telluride ski resort. This was a place chosen for its predictability. Getting it right meant solving a math problem: Calculate the number of bulbs you need to process and how fast you can process them. Count back from Easter to determine your start date and turn the belts on.

Not long before I went to Smith River, I had a conversation with a man named Bill West, who gave me the vocabulary to name what the Easter lily growers were up to. I was about to tour the assembly line that Airbus had built in Mobile, Alabama, where the European conglomerate built airplanes meant for the American market. In terms of size, revenue, and sophistication, Airbus is about as different from a family farm as you can imagine, but the methods they used to deliver their products on time shared a kinship.

West is the head of operations for Airbus Americas Engineering, so he spends a lot of time thinking about schedules and planning. He is one small part of a giant operation—his specialty is wing structures—but he knows how to keep his eye on a deadline. "Once I tell JetBlue I'm going to deliver an airplane on the fifteenth of December of this year, it's got to be delivered on that date," he told me. At the assembly line in Mobile, a new Airbus A320, a single-aisle aircraft meant to compete with the Boeing 737, rolls off the line every six days.

The assembly line, though, is only the final stretch of what can be a ten-year process from the initial development of the aircraft to FAA certification to production. It costs about $15 billion to see it all the way through. "You build the schedule backward—right to left, as we call it," he told me. Just like the lily growers, you determine your deadline and count back in time from there. You map out how much time you need for each stage of the process (whether it's vernalizing the bulbs or designing a new wing shape) and then set your start date. Try things the other way—left to right—and you're inviting a never-ending series of time and cost overruns. Or, if you're a lily farmer, you don't have any flowers on Easter. It's so simple it sounds like a tautology: having a deadline makes it possible to meet the deadline.

Mobile is a working port, accustomed to the sight of dry-docks and shipping cranes bumping up against the city's homes and office buildings, but still it was strange to see just how close Airbus's massive facility is from the city center. Three miles: the distance from Times Square to SoHo. The hangars for the A320 were located at 320 Airbus Way. Soon they will also start making A220s in Mobile, and that facility will sit at—where else—220 Airbus Way.

An Airbus employee named Kristi Tucker showed me the giant hangar, called the final assembly line (FAL), where workers were building the A320s. Each building on campus was numbered, Tucker told me, but not sequentially. Instead, they copied the numbers from the original A320 campus in Hamburg, which meant that I could see an 8, 9, 10, 12, and 19, but no buildings to fill those gaps. (Keeping numbering consistent allowed for easy communication with Europe. The FAL in both cities, for example, was in building 9.)

The FAL hangar had the deadly still, perfect feeling of the inside of a domed stadium, minus the people and the noise. We walked up to third-floor catwalk to look down at the planes taking shape below. There are four stations inside the building: 41, where workers join the two halves of the fuselage; 40, where they add the wings and landing gear; 35, where they put the tail in place; and the dock, where the engines go on. The numbers represent the number of days the plane is from delivery, or they used to until Airbus made the whole process faster. "We've gotten leaner and meaner," said Tucker. At each station there was a clock counting down until each plane was meant to move to the next station. At that moment it read 2 days, 4 hours, 15 minutes, 32 seconds.

Before workers join the fuselage at 41, they install the lavatories and galleys in the open ends. These pre-assembled pieces are known collectively as "monuments." To get from 41 to 40, the fuselage flies through air, suspended by a crane attached to the ceiling. After 40, the plane rolls on its own wheels. Tucker said that the FAL in Hamburg looks identical to this, except the crane here is painted yellow rather than orange.

At station 40, workers used an arched stairway to climb over the center of the plane. They were installing the wings, the most intricate part of the process, involving 1,200 rivets, with their placement measured to within one tenth of a millimeter. To speed up the line, a second set of wings and pylons were sitting under the installed wings, ready for the next fuselage to come along, like a batter stepping to the plate from the on-deck circle.

The vertical stabilizers came pre-painted, so once the plane reached station 35, you could tell who the customer was. An aircraft meant for Delta was at station 35, and one meant for Frontier was in the dock. Airbus installs third-party equipment at the dock station, including the seats, which the airline can pick out of a catalog. At this point, the plane is close enough to delivery that workers have to wear special pocketless clothing and booties to keep from scratching it.

From the FAL, the plane moves on to gauging, to test the fuel tanks, and then to the paint shop. It takes seven to ten days to paint a plane. Then it goes to the flight line hangar, where every component is tested before the plane flies for the first time. Airbus keeps a staff of test pilots in Mobile, who put the plane through stresses beyond what normal operations would require.

After Airbus completes its tests, the airlines bring in their own pilots for a "consumer acceptance flight." The whole delivery process takes four days, including test flights and title transfers. The delivery center has parking spaces for five aircraft—one for each plane the line produces each month. The final day is the transfer-of-title date. The airline wires the money to Airbus and takes possession of the aircraft. Now it is theirs.

So: it took me a thousand words just to describe the last forty days or so of a ten-year process. Managing all that complexity, from Bill West's drafting board to final delivery, requires a system. And it all begins with scheduling everything right to left.

Many of the men and women I met in Easter lily country had committed to memory a potted history of the industry, ready to unleash on a visitor. Crockett launched into a version of it within minutes of our first meeting at the Farm Bureau.

Usually the story picks up during the Second World War, and for good reason, but I'm going to start even earlier, with the late-eighteenth-century "discovery" of the lily in Japan by a Swedish naturalist named Carl Peter Thunberg. Like most Europeans in Japan at the time, Thunberg was confined to Dejima, an artificial island off the coast of Nagasaki, and his interactions with the Japanese were restricted. After he proved adept at treating syphilis, however, the Japanese gave him permission to explore some parts of the mainland, where he collected plant samples. One of these was *lilium longiflorum*.

By the mid-nineteenth century, the flower had made its way to Bermuda, where it had the useful habit of blooming in early spring. Harry Harms, the grower from Hastings Inc., attributed the spread of the flower in the United States to a Philadelphia florist who visited Bermuda on vacation: "He saw these things blooming there at about Easter time and said 'Shit, I can sell the hell out of those.'" (Like most origin stories, this one seems to be a mixture of fact and fiction.) For decades Bermuda lilies dominated the US market, long enough to establish the flower as the standard accompaniment for

Easter church services or on the dining table at Easter luncheon. When a virus wiped out the island's crop in the 1890s, Japanese growers stepped up to meet demand, and the market in Bermuda never recovered. (The island still sends a batch of lilies to Buckingham Palace every year, however, as an Easter gift to the queen.)

Between the wars, Japan shipped 20 million to 25 million lilies to the United States every year. The attack on Pearl Harbor, of course, ended imports, and the price of lilies jumped. Farmers in California and Oregon were already growing a hardy cultivar in small batches and in garden plots. Once the price climbed toward a dollar a bulb, these plants moved from the margins to center stage. Lily farms popped up from Portland to Santa Cruz. At one point, there were as many as 1,200 commercial growers on the West Coast.

The story ever since then has been one of consolidation, first as a sign of strength, as cash-rich growers bought each other out, and then of weakness, as rising costs and falling prices led farmers to look for any efficiencies they could uncover. A lot of my conversations with the lily growers were about how much longer the business could survive. Not long, was the consensus. "We used to call the bulbs white gold," said June Markum, the office manager at Hastings. "We don't call them that anymore."

The Hastings operation is right up against the water, on a high cliff over the ocean. The office itself is covered in faux wood paneling and looks like it hasn't been updated since *Dallas* was on the air, but through the window the blue Pacific was almost blindingly bright. Year after year, Markum told me, she faced two big challenges: hiring enough people to harvest and process the bulbs, and getting enough trucks to come to the coast to pick them up. Finding a reliable workforce had been especially difficult lately. Locals didn't want the job, and migrant farmworkers had been slowly squeezed out by three decades of immigration crackdowns. She showed me a thick folder with the applications of people who had worked the line and then dropped out. On the top of one application, someone had written "TOO ANXIOUS TO WORK." As for trucks, they needed about two hundred semis a season. But because the farm was hours from the nearest interstate and there wasn't a lot of other business for a shipper to do in the area, the trucks were required to deadhead there to pick up the lilies, which cost extra.

Markum said the four remaining growers were eyeing their competitors closely: "We're waiting to see who's next to drop off." But she also insisted that at Hastings they wanted everyone to survive: "We like to keep the little guys going, because they are family businesses." She pulled a laminated page off the wall. It showed the date of Easter for every year from 1996 to 2045, when I suppose they'll have to print a new cheat sheet for the next half century, if Hastings is still around.

Harry Harms arrived, and he took over where Markum left off. He said that for all the troubles the lily growers faced, they were more efficient than they had ever been. No one ever missed a deadline anymore. There had been innovations: new cultivars, sprays that prevented botrytis or nematodes, the decision to snip the buds off before they bloomed to maximize bulb size. "Our ability to control things is just hugely better than it used to be," Harms said. "It was all art back in the day to get this Easter bloom. Freaking smoke and mirrors is all it was." They got the timing dialed in, from harvest to cooling to greenhouse to final sale, and the plant itself became increasingly standardized. Five blooms, 24 inches tall, ready to go.

Their ability to deliver on deadline wasn't the problem; it was their inability to exert any control over price. That was mainly an effect of the big-box stores taking over most of their business. If Home Depot or Walmart decided that an Easter lily was going to sell for eight dollars instead of ten dollars, there was little the farmers could do about it. "It's been our demise," Harms said. "It's what's going to put us out of business. It's what's putting us out of business. When the biggest retailer in the world has on every one of his buildings, 'Always the Lowest Price' who do you think loses? The vendors. The vendors get crushed. Actually, and in all fairness, Walmart's not the worst. Other big boxes are frigging brutal." Harms had also seen the disappearance of the seasonal labor force that the industry used to depend on. "Crew here is everything and we cannot get enough crew," he said. Before the border was so heavily policed, farmers up and down California could get laborers to pick strawberries and cherries, move on to tomatoes, pick up specialty crops like Easter lilies in the fall, and then head south for oranges in the winter. The workers would come from Mexico to work for a year or two and then return home with cash in hand to start a business or build a house. Now those same immigrants were more likely to remain in the United States rather than risk another crossing, which meant they were looking for jobs that allowed them to stay in one place and set up a life. Specialized crops like the Easter lily had lost their workforce.

The result was a system in which any labor-intensive crops became increasingly difficult to produce, while mechanized operations thrived. "If you want to eat beans, rice, soybeans, corn, and barley your whole frickin' life, you're in the right place, but if you want to have a cherry or a cucumber or anything like that, you're out of luck," Harms said. "Agriculture is dying. Agriculture is weak. It's happening really fast in front of our eyes."

Underlying his anger was a steadfast love for the crop he'd devoted his life to. He spoke of the lily, its beauty and its fragility, with something approaching tenderness. He also said that from a moneymaking standpoint, everyone should have left the business by now, but they were all "addicted." He missed the days when they just let the flowers bloom.

Back at Westbrook, workers were still packing lily bulbs, nail-gunning boxes together, loading pallets of them onto a forklift to move into the storage building. Crockett asked me if I wanted to meet Will Westbrook, who owns and operates Palmer Westbrook with his brother Matt. We found him standing near the end of the line, next to the control box that turned the belt off and on. Will Westbrook was in his forties but looked a lot younger, with a sturdy frame, a sunburnt face, and a ball cap on. There was dirt under his fingernails from picking bulbs off the line to inspect them.

Westbrook said he'd be happy to talk, but he'd have to keep his eye on the clock. "We have fourteen minutes until the buzzer rings for lunch," he said, at which point the workers would walk away from the line whether it was still moving or not. His margins were already incredibly tight, and he couldn't afford to lose any bulbs. Many of his best workers had been driven away by the Trump administration's immigration policy, and those who remained were getting paid well, thanks to California's minimum wage law, which he accepted with a sort of fatalism: "Overtime for minimum wage is, what, eighteen dollars? Wow, that's the first time I've said that out loud." He shook his head.

Westbrook was unabashed about what would help him now. "I would love to find some robots that knew how to sort lilies," he said. The Dutch, masters of all things in the flower world, had an automated sorter that could replace his apple grader, but it was built for tulips, which are hardier than lily bulbs. He couldn't afford to purchase one anyway. I was reminded of something Harms had told me: "That's the whole goal of capitalism: to make sure nobody's got a job."

Westbrook may have dreamed about Dutch robots, but in the meantime he was treating his workers well enough to keep them coming back year after year. Even as other operations had to churn through applications to keep their line staffed, Westbrook had held on to some veteran sorters, mostly transplants from Mexico who had first started working for his father and his uncle back when it was easier for migrant farmworkers to move from job to job.

As the clock ticked down to twelve-thirty, when the buzzer would make a sound like a cellblock being opened, Westbrook walked over to the conveyor controls. Crockett appeared from her hiding spot as the buzzer echoed through the shed. Westbrook hit the stop button, the machines froze, and everyone ran to the microwaves to heat up their lunches. Once the line stopped, Westbrook locked the control box to keep someone from turning it back while they cleaned the machinery. Crockett told a story about one of her workers at Crockett United who lost a finger when someone turned on the belts while it was being repaired. Westbrook looked at me and said, "You're welcome to go wherever you want, but try not to lose a finger."

Outside, the line workers were sitting on their truck tailgates and car bumpers eating their lunches. One of the employees, a man named Filemon, took me to look at the "dropper," the tractor they used for planting. It had a rig on it that could till the soil and place bulbs at regular intervals, all at a walking pace. A commercial bulb usually got its start as "scale," a single clove that would mature into a walnut-sized bulblet by year's end. The bulblet would be harvested and replanted in October, then harvested again the next year, by which time it would be a proper bulb—but still not large enough to sell commercially. One more year in the ground would usually be enough to bring it up to seven inches or more, but some bulbs require five years to reach that size. Filemon told me he had been working for Westbrook for ten years, ever since he arrived in California from Mexico City. When he started, most of the work was still done by hand, years of digging and replanting, just to get a bulb that would sell for a dollar.

Harvesting had also been partially automated, but it was still tough work. Crockett took me out into the field to watch a line of bulbs get pulled out the ground by the potato-digging rig, which looked like a plywood concession stand being dragged by a tractor. Three or four men—and it was mostly men in the fields—were standing inside the structure as it was pulled along. Another was lying flat on his belly on a little table on wheels that was pulled along like a caboose behind the tractor and the shack. It all looked improbably jury-rigged and tumble-down, but it was the standard tool for the harvest for all four growers. Crockett pulled me up into the shack to show me how it worked.

At the front of the structure, right behind the tractor, there is a scoop that plunges into the soil, pulling up what is down there: in this case, ideally, a bunch of lily bulbs. The bulbs and rocks and whatever else the scoop picks up travels up a short conveyor belt into the shack, where the workers grab the bulbs and throw them onto a parallel conveyor, which dumps the keepers into one of the large wooden boxes that would eventu-ally end up at the start of the sorting line. Whatever they don't throw up on the keeper belt runs off the back of the main con-veyor and falls onto the ground. The guy lying on his belly on his little man-sized trailer—man and trailer both are referred to as a creeper—is there to retrieve any bulbs the other workers accidentally reject.

Even this ramshackle setup is an improvement over the pre-vious harvesting method. When Harms started in the business, he said, there were no potato-digging machines in Smith River. Instead, the workers would crawl on their hands and knees behind the tractor and pick up the bulbs by hand. "You'd pull a box, crawl up a row, and pick the bulbs up," he said. "Fill your box, grab another empty box," and start the whole process again.

The workers in the potato digger were too busy to even glance at me and Crockett. The tractor kept driving and we bumped through the field. To be distracted even for a second would mean letting a bulb go by unrescued, the equivalent of leaving a trail of dollar bills scattered behind the shack.

Planning right to left sounds easy, but it requires people like Linda Crockett and Will Westbrook to overcome a consistent human failing. It's called the planning fallacy.

Amos Tversky and Daniel Kahneman coined the term in 1977, for a paper they wrote about predictions for DARPA, the Defense Advanced Research Projects Agency. Kahneman later said he was inspired in part by the experience he'd had writing a textbook with a group of academics. At the beginning of that project, he had asked the participants to estimate how long it would take. The average guess was two years. It took nine.

Most of us are optimists, which might make us better company at the dinner table, but it means we are lousy at predicting the future. We underestimate the amount of time a project will require. If it's a project that has a budget, we underestimate the expense as well. That was true with the construction of Pier 17, the home of the Fulton; indeed, it's a problem that plagues the building industry generally. The most famous example of this tendency is probably the Sydney Opera House, which was commissioned in 1957 with an expected completion date of 1963 and a budget of $7 million Australian dollars. The building wasn't finished until 1973, and only after the most ambitious versions of the plan had been scaled back, for a final cost of $102 million.

The planning fallacy is the tendency to seize upon the most optimistic timetable for completing a project and ignore any information that might make you revise that prediction. According to Roger Buehler, a professor of psychology at Wilfrid Laurier University, people are pretty stubborn about these conclusions even when presented with evidence of how they've been wrong in the past. Although they are aware that "most of their previous predictions were overly optimistic, they believe that their current forecasts are realistic." Tom DeMarco, a former software engineer at Bell Labs, once said that software completion deadlines were "the most optimistic prediction that has a nonzero probability of coming true."

Buehler and some colleagues at the University of Waterloo in Ontario ran a test on their students to see how bad they were at estimating when they would finish their work. They asked thirty-seven seniors to make three predictions: the date they would submit their honors thesis "if everything went as well as it possibly could," the date "if everything went as poorly as it possibly could," and their best guess for what their actual submission date would be.

Fewer than 30 percent submitted their work by the date they thought was the best estimate of when they would be done. The optimistic predictions were even worse—they were off by an average of 28 days, and barely 10 percent of the students were done by that date. The most striking result, however, might be the one for the pessimistic scenario. Even when asked to predict what would happen "if everything went as poorly as it possibly could," the students were still too optimistic. Fewer than half had finished by the worst-case-scenario date.

The problem with our predictions is that we treat each task like it's a novel problem. We can only see from left to right: we construct a story about how we will complete our work but ignore evidence from similar projects we or other people have done in the past. That was true with Kahneman's textbook: One of the academics admitted that earlier projects he'd worked on took a minimum of seven years. But when it was time to estimate how long this one would take, he guessed two years like everyone else.

It's not all hopeless, though. There is a way to overcome, or at least mitigate, the planning fallacy. In a follow-up experiment, Buehler and his colleagues had a different group of students complete a one-hour computer tutorial at some point before a one-' or two-week deadline. They also asked them to predict when they would finish the assignment, but here the researchers inserted a variable. Some of the students were prompted to think about past assignments they had completed that were similar to this one, and to apply that knowledge to their prediction. The control group was given no such instructions.

The results were remarkable: although the control group exhibited the same optimistic bias as the students in the first experiment, that bias almost disappeared among the students who were prompted to forge a connection between their past experiences and the current assignment. They predicted it would take them an average of seven days to complete the tutorial. The actual average: seven days.

In the office at Hastings, there was a reason that a calendar dating back to 1996 was up on the wall. The farmers were bound by the Easter deadline—they couldn't afford to let the planning fallacy have its way with them. So they did what those students did, only without the prodding of a group of professors. They took their past experience and used it to build a schedule, planning right to left, counting back from Easter. They knew down to the day how long the lilies had to be in greenhouses, how long in storage, and how long it took to get them out of the ground and into boxes. And if anyone had a question about how things had worked the last time Easter fell on, say, April 20, they could easily get an answer. After all, these were family farms: there were multiple generations on hand, and they had seen it all before.

The week before I arrived in Smith River, Sonny Perdue, the secretary of agriculture, held a town hall at the World Dairy Expo in Wisconsin. The state had been losing an average of 900 dairy farms a year for decades, as family farms got bought up by conglomerates or just went out of business. Fewer than 8,000 were left, in a state that once had more than 130,000. Someone asked Perdue about these vanishing farms, and he declined to offer false comfort to farmers who couldn't adapt. "In America," he said, "the big get bigger and the small go out."

The risk Harry Harms saw in that trend was that these bigger ag companies might decide that certain crops weren't worth growing at all. Why bother with the multiyear, labor-intensive process to get a bulb ready to bloom when the whole industry brought in around $10 million in revenue, and a fraction of that in profit? Small growers were the only reason Easter lilies still existed at all, and there was no telling how much longer that would last.

Back on the line, Westbrook was taking his tape measure to a few of the rejects rolling down the belt. Without his intervention, they would wind up in a bin, destined either to be replanted or composted. He grabbed one and looped the tape measure around it. The numbers on the tape had all worn off, but he'd hand-drawn a line for seven, eight, and nine inches in permanent marker. This one was just past the seven line, but he let it go to the reject pile anyway, perhaps because I was standing there.

Westbrook got ready for the 4:30 buzzer, when he would shut down the line for the day. By running from 7:00 to 4:30, he was paying one hour of overtime daily. That was the balance he and his brother had struck, at least for now, between keeping payroll down and getting the bulbs packed in time to start their long journey to Easter. The first trucks of the season had come and gone two days before, and the next one would arrive tomorrow. They were in the heart of the hardest part, Westbrook said.

As we talked, Crockett threw a bulb at Westbrook, which just missed his head. "You never know when a bulb fight is going to break out," he said. The workers on the line were scrambling as quickly as ever to get the bulbs in the right place at the right time, though I saw a few glance at the clock. As the seconds ticked down to 4:30, Westbrook put a few tiny boxes of Milk Duds on the belt, where they floated down to be picked off by the sorters, a surprise treat at quitting time.

When the buzzer rang, Westbrook went to talk to his brother, and Crockett and I stepped outside the shed. Maybe it was the weariness of day's end, or maybe she'd warmed up to me, but she finally seemed eager to talk. She had always loved farming, she said, and she loved Easter lilies in particular. By this point she had tried every job on the farm, from the payroll office to the creeper. The rift with her brother was only the latest in a lifetime of feeling pushed aside on the farm. "Growing up, because I was a woman, I couldn't drive the tractor," she said. "But I wanted to." She believes that Crockett United is suffering without her.

At this point, her whole life has been devoted to the lily. It was a difficult crop, almost too difficult to bother with, but that was what kept her interested. She said that when she was younger, every day she and her dad would sit on the back porch after work and talk. He had a big portfolio to manage—timber, dairy, real estate, stocks—and he had quit overseeing the lilies day to day. But still, whenever they sat on the porch, that's all he wanted to talk about with her. "How are those lilies doing?" he asked.

3

A Soft Open
with Teeth: Telluride
Ski Mountain

It was November 15, 2018, and Telluride didn't look anything like a ski mountain. The runs were dirty and brown. They resembled the lifeless gullies of the LA River more than a snow-covered meadow. There were a few whale-sized lumps of snow scattered about, but the lifts were locked in place, and the streets in town were almost empty.

Through the cold, a group of about ninety men and women—the senior staff of Telluride—walked toward a conference center not far from the slopes. This was the crew that would open the mountain for the year, and they had one week to do it. Or that was the plan, at least: for decades, Telluride had opened on Thanksgiving Day, and everyone, from the families who had already booked their hotel rooms to the businesses in town that depended on tourism to survive, was counting on that tradition continuing.

In the past, the employees of Telluride may have been able to wait for the snow to fall and cover the slopes naturally, but in the twenty-first century, they had a few more tools at their disposal. Those mounds of snow on the otherwise bone-dry runs were the product of multiple nights of snowmaking—there was a team working from sundown to sunup every time the temperature dropped below freezing, pointing water cannons at the sky.

Man-made snow, not just at Telluride but at every big resort, has saved the multi-billion-dollar ski industry from the extremes of climate change—in which a year of record snowfall can be followed by an absolute drought—but it comes at a cost. Bill Jensen, the CEO of Telluride, plans to spend $15 million on snowmaking over the next ten years. "The next five years could be great snow years," he said, "but this way we don't have to worry."

Meeting that Thanksgiving deadline was important not because it was hugely profitable for the resort itself—the thousand skiers they expected was a fraction of the eight thousand a day that would come the week after Christmas—but because it set the tone for the entire season. "Traditionally," Jensen said, "on that Thanksgiving holiday, there's a family discussion." Parents, grandparents, and children are all gathered together, and they are planning their vacations, especially for the end of the year and for spring break. If Telluride is closed that day, it sends a message: we won't be ready for you if you come.

Jensen's competition was intense, and on the lookout for just such a slipup. Over the past few years, most of the big mountains in North America had sold to one of two corporations, Vail Resorts and Alterra Mountain Company. Telluride, with annual revenue of about $80 million, was one of the few remaining independents of any size. Vail Resorts' revenue alone was more than $2 billion, and they could invest hundreds of millions of dollars in their properties. Both companies were eager to poach the big-spending destination skiers that Telluride attracted to Colorado.

As it happened, Vail had opened early in 2018: the first skiers hit the slopes on November 14. At Telluride that day, as we know—the LA River. The sharks' teeth of the San Juan Mountains loomed overhead, coated in white, like a reproach.

The first time we spoke, in mid-October, Jensen didn't know whether they could make enough snow before Thanksgiving to allow them to open on time. They needed 200 hours of cold dry weather just to cover the slopes around chair 1 and chair 4, the two lifts at the base of the main mountain. "If it will just be twenty degrees every night starting next week, yes, we'll be open," he said, but there was a weariness to his voice. Forty-four years in the ski industry and he was still looking at the sky and hoping.

It was brave, then, for Jensen to invite me out to Telluride to watch the final ramp-up to opening day. Thanksgiving 2018 was on November 22, the earliest it could possibly be—he'd have six fewer days (or, as Jensen put it, seventy to eighty hours of missing snowmaking time) to get everything ready compared to the following year.

Even when the weather cooperated, it was still a huge operation to start up each year. The staff would more than double in size. "We are waking up a ski resort," Heather Young, the director of human resources, said. "We go from about six hundred employees up to about fourteen hundred. We see anywhere from twenty to fifty people a day joining the staff through the first of the year." There were twelve restaurants to open. Dozens of lift operators to train. Thousands of acres of mountain to patrol. A ski school to staff. And, most important, a whole mountain of snow to make and push onto the slopes.

It would be a mad dash to the finish, but Jensen and his staff had a secret weapon, one that drew its power from the very nature of opening on Thanksgiving. They had set a deadline that gave every impression of being a make-or-break event: people would be showing up at the mountain that day expecting to ski. But really it was a soft open posing as a hard deadline. The *true* deadline, the one that would wreck the season if they couldn't meet it, was the week after Christmas, which represented 20 percent of the skier visits for the year.

"I've used this analogy my whole career," Jensen said. "Opening this ski area is like wrapping a Christmas present. For Thanksgiving, all we had to do is get the present in the box. On December 8th, I'd like to have the box wrapped with some nice wrapping paper. Somewhere around December 18th to 20th, let's put the ribbon on that package and we're ready to go." Indeed, there was even a soft open to the soft open: the resort would allow skiers on a limited number of runs on the day before Thanksgiving for something called Donation Day, in which all lift-ticket sales would go to benefit the local kids' ski club.

Telluride had created the same conditions for itself that Jean-Georges Vongerichten had achieved at his friends and family dinners, and what I had tried to create for pathologically tardy writers such as John: a soft deadline with teeth. It was a way of gaining the virtues of the deadline effect (focus, urgency, cooperation) with none of the vices (rashness, desperation, incompleteness).

In the introduction to this book, we learned about Kiva, a nonprofit lender to small businesses, which saw a 24 percent increase in completed loan applications after imposing a deadline. Kiva later ran a second experiment. They told prospective borrowers that their application would be given priority if they met a soft deadline six days before the final cutoff. The result? Completed applications rose by an additional 26 percent—a

56 percent total increase compared to when Kiva imposed no deadline at all.

At Telluride, Jensen knew that the world wouldn't end if they couldn't open on Thanksgiving. But if they made it, they'd be positioned to nail the far more consequential deadline of the Christmas holidays. The wisdom of this schedule had been borne out by the past two years, when the weather was so warm in the early season that they couldn't open on Thanksgiving. In 2016 they missed the deadline by a few days. The following year, they missed it by a few weeks—they were barely able to open for Christmas, in fact—and then the whole season was rotten. It was too warm. It didn't snow. They had trouble keeping terrain open, and skier visits were way down. "It was a challenging year," Jensen told me. "We couldn't get it done." Heather Young claimed that she had blocked out the memory of last Thanksgiving: "Like childbirth, you forget in order to protect yourself."

But even the failures of 2017 were undoubtedly mitigated by the goal of opening at Thanksgiving. Jensen couldn't control the weather, but he could set deadlines and motivate his staff to make the best of whatever came their way. If Telluride had been planning to open on, say, December 15 of that year, and they had delayed snowmaking and all the rest accordingly, the slopes would have been barren at Christmas. That's the brilliance of using soft deadlines to your advantage: the worst-case scenarios become survivable, and you're poised to capitalize mightily on anything better than that.

The trick was to treat the soft deadline with seriousness. Jensen had already made the most important move—keeping the opening early—but it was up to the staff to harness the deadline effect across the mountain's many interlocking parts. Only if the employees in every division thought of Thanksgiving as a hard deadline would it all work.

The early evidence was promising: at that season-opening

managers' meeting on November 15, the mood was buoyant but determined. Most of the staff there were in their twenties and thirties, wearing puffy zip-up jackets over flannel shirts. They looked simultaneously wholesome and grungy, like the black sheep in a Mormon family. When Jensen took the stage, they sat at attention and the room fell silent.

Jensen is in his sixties, with watery blue eyes, thin gray hair, and a jolly look on his face. His speech to the group was basically a forty-five-minute pep talk meant to dispel the memory of the 2017 season. "Last year was a blip on the radar screen," he said. In Colorado, they expect to be starved for snow one year out of every ten, so the dire season wasn't exactly unprecedented. Still, he said, "I hope we have a nice nine-year run now."

I wondered why Jensen was dwelling so long on 2017, but then I realized that after two years of missing the Thanksgiving deadline, he knew he had to reaffirm both that it was possible and that it was the staff's responsibility to make it so. The stakes were suitably high: the previous year led to a 50 percent drop in profits. They had navigated the crisis without having to lay anyone off— indeed, they had increased employee pay. But they couldn't keep doing that if they kept missing deadlines and losing skiers. Jensen put the matter succinctly: "This year we have to recover."

———

With six days to go until Thanksgiving, I sat down with Jeff Proteau, the vice president of mountain operations and planning, in an office filled with flat files and binders, the product of thirty years spent negotiating the care and feeding of a ski resort. It was cloudless and cold, and even though the sun was up, there were five guns shooting snow into the air on Misty Maiden, the wide ski run that dead-ends right into the heart of town.

Proteau was taking the deadline seriously. His plan was to open two "pods" on the first day: chairs 1 and 4 and the multiple runs that surrounded them, which represented a sizable chunk of Telluride's 2,000 acres of skiable terrain. It was an area bigger than the whole of most resorts on the East Coast. After opening day, the snowmakers would get to work on the rest of the mountain, with the aim of getting it open within another two weeks—well before Christmas.

Proteau is short and powerfully built, like someone who had spent a lot of time troubleshooting problems that occasionally involved moving heavy gear around. "My job is to be in front of everybody else making sure that everything they need is there when they need it," he said. A few years ago, Telluride had opened up hundreds of acres of new terrain on the upper part of the mountain, all the way to the top of Palmyra Peak, which stands at 13,320 feet. It was an enormous endeavor, one that required coordinating with the local, state, and federal governments. "All those notebooks you see right there, that's what it took to go through and analyze this from every angle you can imagine," he said. "Everything from the fritillary butterfly to the avalanches that could occur out here. We had to know everything." The notebooks had names like AVALANCHE, GEOLOGY AND SOILS, VEGETATION/WETLANDS, LAND USE, HYDROLOGY, and, last, APPEALS printed on their sides.

When Proteau arrived at Telluride, it was a mom-and-pop operation. "It was a little rundown, to be honest with you," he said. No snowmaking, a handful of lifts, completely at the mercy of the weather. That all had changed. Now they had the ability to convert 5,000 gallons of water into snow every hour if the weather got cold enough.

Not that he was ignoring natural snowfall: they needed that once they built the base of artificial snow. To urge on what nature wouldn't provide, they had cloud-seeding sites spread out to the west of us. These were remote-controlled cannons on mountaintops that could shoot silver iodide into the atmosphere, urging the clouds to leave as much of themselves behind as possible as they passed through the San Juans. That operation required a weather-modification permit from the state—another binder in Proteau's office.

Both the snowmaking and the cloud seeding were responses to twin forces in the industry: the rise of skiing as a multi-billion-dollar business and the volatile weather brought by climate change. The first created a client base that expected consistency and high quality. The latter made those very things harder to achieve. Proteau said that Telluride's high elevation (its highest peak is 2,000 feet higher than Vail's, for example) somewhat protected it from rising temperatures, but he would be nervous if he had to run a resort any closer to sea level. As it was, climate experts were predicting that the length of the ski season would be cut in half for some of the most vulnerable areas.

Proteau introduced me to his deputy, Scott Pittenger, who would take me out on a snowmobile to see what they had accomplished in the weeks they'd been "building the mountain." Pittenger, like Proteau, was an Indiana boy who came out to Colorado and got stuck, hooked for life after a single ski season. He was tall and lanky, with a Midwestern aw-shucks quality just barely inflected with a western stoner vibe. (At one point he would tell me he was confident the mountain would open in time because "the stoke level is high.")

Our first stop on Pittenger's snowmobile was a beginner area called Meadows. The big challenge here was making the whole expanse, which doubles as a golf course driving range in the summer, as flat as possible. That meant taking the shelves and slopes of the tee boxes and spackling over them with snow. Pittenger drove us through a thin white strip that had already been filled in, but there were wide swaths of grass still waiting for the snowmakers to arrive.

From the lower mountain, we headed up to "the shop," three

buildings with corrugated steel sides hidden in the woods near the top of chair 4. This was the headquarters for snowmaking, grooming, and vehicle maintenance. There were eighteen snow-cats here, little heated carapaces perched on top of tank tracks, which do everything from hauling food up to the restaurants to moving snow around the mountain. Zooming around everywhere were men and women on snowmobiles. During the pre-season, every machine was dedicated, one way or another, to making snow. Pittenger moved us to a cat to make the climb to the top of Palmyra Peak.

We rode along on white highways laid atop brown hills. The higher we went, the fewer people we saw: the staff was concentrating all its efforts on getting the lower mountain in shape. Once we got on a run called See Forever, which ran along a ridgeline all the way to the top of the highest lift, at 12,500 feet, we were all alone.

There had been natural snowfall up here, and Pittenger was zealous about protecting it. At one point, we had to cross a patch of red dirt. When we got back on the snow, Pittenger made the cat do a little shimmy back and forth to clean off the tracks. Nothing burns away a snowpack faster than rocks and dirt, he said. They are referred to as "disease" in the snow because of how effectively they absorb heat and melt everything around them.

Pittenger said natural snow was almost always welcome, but early in the season, it was actually better to lay down a base layer of man-made snow, which was denser and melted slower. Under his direction, the grooming crews had been pushing as much snow as possible into high-traffic areas—at the bottoms and tops of lifts, on narrow roads that connected one area to another, along the path to the midmountain operations base. He had hard-won knowledge from the past two years about which tasks were vital to getting the mountain open and which could wait. In meeting after meeting, I saw that Pittenger was brilliant at just what the moment required: sending a message of urgency to the staff, while still maintaining an upbeat, we're-all-in-this-together spirit.

Pittenger's daughter had been born in the middle of the ski season four years ago, during a blizzard, and they were expecting another on December 10—right in the heart of Telluride's post-opening Christmas prep. His wife knew better than to expect him to take much paternity leave during ski season. Until the baby arrived, he was working 6:00 am to 6:00 pm every day.

The terrain got steeper, with trees standing at acute angles to the ground. We saw slopes where the ski patrol had side-stepped down the mountain to compact the natural snow. A base of untouched powder could "rot," hollowing out in the sun and wind, which made it prone to avalanches. The patrol was painstakingly turning that powder into a denser base, mimicking the conditions produced by snowmaking equipment. The goal was to "preserve every snowflake."

The trees disappeared and the ridgeline shrank to the width of our snowcat. On either side, the mountain dropped sharply away, and at certain turns we had to stick the front blade or rear tiller of the cat out over the abyss. It was terrifying.

Close to the top, we passed signs that said CLOSED: EXPLOSIVES IN USE. We were well into avalanche-control territory, where the ski patrol would regularly dynamite slopes to prevent buildups that could lead to slides.

Finally, the road ended and there were only the jagged rocks of Palmyra Peak above us. We scrambled up some snow-covered boulders till we could go no further. Below our feet were the highest reaches of the Telluride ski area. Everything looked murderously steep, and it was so vast you couldn't take it in all at once. This was the task facing Pittenger and his team.

Back in town, ski instructors were trying out new uniforms, ticket takers were learning how to operate the scanner guns, food workers were memorizing the new menus, and lifties were filling out their first W-4s. None of it would matter, however, if there wasn't enough snow on the slopes. The small crew making all that snow, working mostly at night, was the red-hot center of everything going on at Telluride that week. "Right now," Pittenger told me, "snowmaking owns the mountain."

Four days before the open, I embedded with them for one long day to see what that looked like on the ground. I was one of fifteen working swing shift, 10:00 a.m. to 10:00 p.m., at which point the team for the twelve-hour graveyard shift took over. I began the morning with Brandon Green, director of snowmaking, who was standing in the middle of Misty, flying a drone overhead to make a record of the previous night's work. There were giant wales of snow around us, each of which would be allowed to leach moisture for a day before being spread out by the grooming team. That was the whole process: the snowmakers made a mound of snow, and the groomers pushed it out, over and over again, until they had a finished run.

The drone was Green's idea, after seeing how well it worked for his wife's wedding-photography business. The footage he captured would be screened at the 11:00 a.m. shift-change meeting to show his foremen as precisely and visually as possible where the snowmaking equipment was now and where he wanted it to go.

Everyone I talked to at Telluride, from Jensen on down to the food and beverage workers, described Green as a genius. On first meeting, though, he was tetchy and reserved, and busy as hell. He kept bounding from one side of the slope to the other with no explanation, pausing occasionally to roll another cigarette. He was bearded and compact, with reddish blond hair and a wind-burnt face. Like Pittenger, he sent a signal of urgency to his staff, but it was all in his actions rather than his words.

Several of the snowmakers coming off the clock hung around in the shop for the shift-change meeting, drinking Rainier beer and looking exhausted. They were a scruffy lot, most of them in their twenties. Green went through a weather update, skipping past the snowfall forecast (there were a few inches expected on Thanksgiving itself) and zeroing in on the temperature and humidity data. The colder and drier the air, the more snow they could make. Green described the conditions as "marginal"—meaning not cold enough to turn the guns on full blast—but they would be able to produce new wales every night for the foreseeable future.

Before the meeting ended, Green opened up a folder on his computer labeled "Winter 2017/2018 Worst Ever." This contained the drone footage he shot last year, when they could barely make any snow before December: "A history lesson," he said. The snowmakers made disgusted noises as the drone flew over patchy slopes, red mud and melting snow everywhere. One guy suggested that, rather than a chairlift, it would have been faster to take a Honda Civic to the top.

Last year, the snowmakers kept working through February, the longest Telluride had ever kept them. Green always works more or less without a break during snowmaking season—"I don't think we'll ever get Brandon to work five days a week," Pittenger said—but last season he took to sleeping in his office between shifts. He built a little bench for himself for just that purpose. "They were a tired group of individuals by the end," Jensen told me.

This year, Green was clocking in for a more reasonable stretch of 7:00 a.m. to midnight daily. The most intense part of the action came just after nightfall, when the whole system came online and the first guns started spraying out snow. With just a few days to open, the pace was even more frantic than usual.

Green had a zippy one-person snowmobile that he used to

great effect, darting from one snowmaking gun to the next, making adjustments on the fly. For most of the night I was with the snowmaking crew, I rode behind Pittenger, who tagged along pokily, sometimes losing Green for whole stretches of time.

At one point well after dark, Green had to go back to the shop, and he suggested that I ride with him "Canadian style," which turned out to mean side by side, standing up, each of us holding one handlebar. Green controlled the throttle, and he didn't let the uneven conditions and near pitch-black slow him down. He kept yelling things to me over the roar of the engine, but my brain wouldn't let any information through other than "Must. Not. Let. Go."

Once the temperature dropped below the threshold for making snow (the so-called wet-bulb temperature, a number that changed depending on the relative humidity), we went to the pump house to start sending water from a pair of reservoirs down to the more than 60 guns that would be spraying snow tonight. (Telluride owns 180 guns, but there's not enough water to fire them all at once.) The snowmakers thought of their jobs mainly in terms of water. Green didn't talk about the slopes he had left to cover, he talked volume: "I've pumped forty million gallons so far this season and I've got to pump eighty million more."

What kept Green nervous were the limits imposed by the reservoirs, which took five times as long to refill as they did to empty. He had tapped into the town's fire-hydrant system for some extra volume, but even that only allowed him an extra gun or two. The result was that even in a good season, making enough snow to cover an opening tended to go down to the wire.

With the water pumping, we set out across the mountain again, checking on the guns one by one, making sure they were pointed in the right direction and dialed in. There were fan guns, which looked like jet engines on wheels, and snow lances, which were long aluminum tubes that sprayed their water high up in the air to give the droplets as much time as possible to freeze as they fell. They were arranged in packs of three, four, five, or six, or spread out along the side of a slope. All of them made use of the same basic principle. Combine pressurized air with water to create a fine mist that would freeze before it hit the ground.

From the pump house, we drove downhill on Misty Maiden, on a snow road carved between giant white mounds, surrounded on both sides by guns showering frozen mist down on us. It was an excellent way to get very cold very fast. Each gun had a light on it, which made them look like a parade of ghosts appearing out of the dark. At the bottom, one of the guns wasn't working, so Green opened up its control panel to see what was wrong. Different power sources required different wiring, and this gun had been phased wrong. Green rewired it on the spot and fired it up.

Down on Meadows, the tee boxes were disappearing under the combined effect of multiple nights of snowmaking and days of snowcat work. Green wanted to finish up that run tonight, so he put six brand-new fan guns in a row, right in the middle of the slope. They were offline, and it fell to us to turn them on. First, we switched on the fans, then we arranged the water hoses feeding them, then we walked down to the hydrants. Green told me to turn them on one by one. I started with a little bit of water, but soon Green told me to turn it to "WFO." He must have seen my blank stare because he quickly clarified: wide fucking open. All the while calls were coming through on the radio from other members of Green's team, about a certain gun not working, or the pressure needing to be precisely calibrated on a set of guns, often by manually opening or closing the hydrants. Around us, guys sped by on snowmobiles to go troubleshoot the next problem.

Once the six pack was online, we went down to inspect

another fan gun that was blinking a yellow warning light—an alarm showing that something was wrong. This one was wired out of phase, too, so Green had to pull out his electricians' tools again. With that one online, we went over to a gun that had a frozen nozzle. Another snowmaker was already there with a blowtorch, trying to thaw it out, but the damage had already been done: the gun had been spraying water on the slope below it, which had set up as a thick sheet of ice.

It was cold getting snow-rained on in the dark. Most of the work of fixing these machines required considerable dexterity, and between that and the need to keep rolling cigarettes, Green rarely kept his gloves on. It was hard to believe he hadn't lost a finger to frostbite by now. I only lasted a few hours with the team before I had to tap out and go warm up—they would work through the night, until ten the next morning.

Before I left Green and his team, he said that I was lucky to have observed a quiet night: it was too warm to fire off most of the guns, and only a few things had gone haywire. To me it seemed like chaos, a freezing scary rough-hewn madhouse, and the work would only get more intense in the days to come, as the deadline marched closer and the mountain remained unfinished. Back in my room, warm when the rest of them were still out there in the cold, I could hear the roar of the snow guns, like a white-noise machine.

Two days before Thanksgiving, there was just barely enough snow on the mountain, maybe, but it was in all the wrong places. Green and his team had deposited wales below every gun, but the trails were still more dirt than snow. The job of turning those wales into a skiable mountain belonged to the grooming team.

At this point in the season, the groomers weren't really grooming. They were pushing. The goal was to get every slope covered with between two and three feet of snow, and even with one day to go till Donation Day there were still plenty of places that needed coverage.

I worked a graveyard shift with Greg Deines, a farmer from nearby Montrose who found work in the winter as a groomer. (His nickname on the mountain was Farm.) It was dead dark and hovering around 8°F outside, but our little cabin of light was warm enough for me to take off my jacket. It was easier to work at night, even during the regular season, Deines said, not just because there were no skiers to worry about, but because the headlights on the cat would make any imperfection in the slope jump out.

Deines showed me his copy of the day's instructions: "Blade aggressively and get our open terrain flat, please!" and "EVERYBODY: Detail edges everywhere. Let's get this mountain fully dialed in and PERFECT!" Clearly the head of grooming had gotten the message of urgency.

Shortly before sunrise, there was a mini-crisis: one of the newbie operators had sprung a hydraulic-oil leak and didn't notice it until he'd tracked it over half the mountain. Deines tried to churn it up with the tiller but it was still visible: a long streak of red in the snow, like someone had dragged a dead body to the top. They would have to make more snow to cover it up.

At about 6:30, Pittenger came on the radio: "Morning, Greg, how's it doing out there?" It might have been my imagination, but it seemed like Pittenger's accent got a shade more country when he talked to Deines. At one point, we passed a cat driven by a groomer named Matt Engler. Pittenger had put me on a day shift with Engler, who was widely regarded as being the best at "pushing out piles," which required a deft hand with the blade on the front of the cat, an intuitive sense of snow depth, and deep knowledge of which places needed the most coverage.

The mounds in front of us were taller than the cat: at each

pass, Engler peeled off a new layer until a giant roller of snow formed in front of the blade. It crashed around the cat like waves before an ocean liner, spilling over the blade or getting swept underneath to be flattened by the tracks and groomed by the tiller.

Engler didn't have much to say about why he was considered one of the best groomers on the mountain—Pittenger called him a "master blader"—but he accepted matter-of-factly that it was true. He took his work seriously and seemed not at all surprised that a reporter might as well. He told me that he learned some of his pushing technique by watching videos of the way avalanches propagate down a hillside.

Groomers at Telluride used to work on each run as a team, which had the effect of hiding the work of weaker groomers. Now a groomer got a chance to own a slope, and Engler's stock had subsequently risen. He had the high-intensity squirreliness of someone who spent all of his working life alone, sealed in a heated, glassed-in cabin.

"I hate it when people come near my machine," he said, and laughed. The back and forth of pushing snow was hypnotic. At first I thought I'd get bored after thirty minutes, but soon I felt like I could stay tucked in there forever. Eventually, I disembarked near the bottom. Once again, I got to quit well before the staff on the mountain, charging hard as ever, even thought about calling it a day.

———

It was difficult to get Pittenger or Proteau or any of the other staff to say it out loud, as if to merely acknowledge their good fortune would end it, but by the night before Donation Day, it was clear the resort would be able to open on time. Whatever celebrations might have been in order were put on hold, though, as the snowmakers and groomers went out for one final push.

The next morning, it was ready: a mountain built by the deadline effect. A group of about one hundred eager skiers waited in line at the base of chair 4, hoping to be one of the first to ski the mountain that season. The earliest had arrived there more than an hour before the lifts started running, and they joined in a countdown as the final minutes ticked by. Finally, at 10:00 a.m., the lifties opened the gate and a roar went up in the crowd.

I took a few laps of the mountain, barely skiing. Just looking at transitions, the edges, where ropes were deployed, scrutinizing the snow quality. The runs were all covered, but the edges dropped off abruptly to the dirt. It definitely felt like early-season skiing, but the crowd didn't seem to mind. There was a light dusting of powder snow on the bottom of Misty, the result of a last-minute bout of snowmaking in the early morning, which felt like a telegram from a carefree, snow-filled future. I spent a moment standing in the sun and marveling at the mountain come alive.

At the bottom of chair 1, after I'd done a snooty inspection of the chunky snow on Meadows, I bumped into Scott Clements, the head of the ski patrol, who was running rope along the edge of the trail. Clements told me that even though the number of skiers is small on Donation Day, the patrol treated it like any other day. "When you're open, you're open: It's got to be buttoned up," he said. One sign that it was a real open? The ski patrol expected to be needed right away. Most injuries, he said, were a result of "excessive motivation": a skier rushing to get to fresh snow, a snowboarder showing off. "Someone will get hurt in the next three days," he said. He seemed almost overcome with gratitude when I told him I would let him get back to work.

At 11:30, ninety minutes into the 2018–19 ski season, I met Scott Pittenger for a coffee near the base of chair 4. He wasn't surprised to hear that Clements seemed a bit more stressed out than usual. "It's always stressful as soon as the public's out there," he said. "Everything changes. You have to look over your shoulder, make sure everything you're doing is high and tight."

Pittenger agreed that the resort was, literally, rough around the edges. "From the middle of all of our runs, everything looks great," he said, "but when you start looking at the nooks and crannies and zoom in on the periphery, then you get a better feeling of what really needs to get done. The detailed stuff doesn't necessarily get lost in the shuffle, but it just isn't the primary focus when a guy gets in a cat and he's like, 'All right, I've got a mountain of snow to move.'" But, he was sure, "It'll look better tomorrow than it did today."

I asked if he regretted opening before the mountain was, as the grooming notes had it, "fully dialed in and PERFECT." Pittenger reminded me that they were serving two crowds at once: the skiers there on the mountain, and the people planning their vacations for the year. He imagined the internal monologues of the second group: "All right, there's snow out there, so we're not going to be kicking around in the dirt on our holiday vacation." The resort would be posting pictures of opening day online, emphasizing that, yes, people were really skiing at Telluride. "It's definitely good for us to be open today and tomorrow. After missing that a couple of years in a row, we definitely took a hit." The radio squawked again, and I saw Pittenger look up impatiently at the mountain. I thanked him and let him go back on the hill to resume his rounds.

At the end of the ski day, the staff crowded into a slopeside bar called Tomboy Tavern, where Telluride was hosting a free-beer happy hour. Bill Jensen had asked all the managers to be here, and everyone made an appearance. Scott Pittenger stopped by for ten seconds before going to attend to the next minor crisis. Jeff Proteau stuck around for a slightly longer visit. When the party wrapped up, Jensen and I went up to his office, directly above the bar. On the way, he picked up an abandoned coffee cup and deposited it in a trash can. It was not the first time I'd seen him pick up a stray bit of garbage.

His office is about the size of a Manhattan Starbucks, with a rustic mustard-brown antique desk and the requisite trail map of the mountain on the wall. There was a giant window that looked out onto the mountain and the bottom of chair 4 and two big computer monitors on his desk, which suggested to me that the room was something more than a showpiece.

It had been Jensen's call to stick to the Thanksgiving schedule after missing the deadline in 2016 and 2017. He said that anything he does on the mountain has to pass the "grocery-store test"—it's such a small town, he'll be called upon to defend anything he decides in person. More than 65 percent of his skiers are returning guests, and he feels a duty to them. Also, among other benefits of hitting the Thanksgiving deadline: since it fell so early in the year, they had an extra week before Christmas to keep making snow, and an extra week to sell tickets. "We'll keep fine-tuning and keep fine-tuning and keep fine-tuning," he said.

"Ultimately, in some ways, it's just putting on a show here, right?" he asked. "It's a Broadway show. Every morning at nine o'clock, the curtain goes up. The groomers are out there at night, we're hauling food to restaurants, we're picking up trash, the snowmakers are working, lift mechanics are coming in at six in the morning to make sure the curtain can go up on time. To be successful at it, you need a team of people that are passionate about what they do."

Jensen told me he only had a few more years left before

he wanted to retire. He had run Breckenridge, Vail, and the multi-mountain conglomerate Intrawest. Telluride was meant to be his swan song. "My primary responsibility here is to build a culture that lasts beyond me," he said. There was some evidence that he was succeeding at that: the staff I spoke to were all eager to quote "Billisms" to me, from the metaphor of getting the Christmas present in the box to his notion of the "final 2 percent" that takes any endeavor from good to great. (As an example of the latter, Jensen pointed out that the staff at Gorrono Ranch Restaurant, which sits below lift 4, had spelled out TELLURIDE using the Adirondack chairs that sat on the deck. "They did that on their own and I love that.") Most important, there was the undeniable dedication from Jensen to Proteau to Pittenger on down to putting in the hard work to meet the early deadline.

Still, the Bill Jensen who picked up an abandoned coffee cup hadn't disappeared. He admitted that he saw more problems today than he expected: "Because of everybody's energy level, I thought maybe we would be just a little bit better, but it's okay." Midmorning, Jeff Proteau came to him with a list of things needing to be fixed. Jensen told him he didn't need to see it. "I said, 'I'll go ski it tomorrow because it'll be better.'"

He had plans to ski in the morning, but because it was Thanksgiving he would be spending most of the day with his family. It was dark outside when we left his office. We said good-bye, after a week together, just in case we didn't see each other on the slopes. As I walked through town, I could hear the snowmakers somewhere, working.

—

Since October I had been busily collecting metaphors about what Thanksgiving really meant to Telluride, whether it was a dress rehearsal, a present in a box or, as the head of ticket sales told me, "a confident crawl" that would soon turn into a run. When opening day itself arrived, it was, by design, an anticlimax. Telluride had proved on Donation Day that it could run skiers on the mountain—what remained was just the everyday work of operating a complex, weather-dependent, multimillion-dollar organization.

I began the day at the lift operations morning meeting, which runs from 7:30 to 8:00, at which point the lifties disperse around the mountain with an hour left to open up their respective chairs. Lift ops headquarters is a shack about the size of a doctor's waiting room, and it's slightly less shabby than you might expect of a place intended to corral as many as forty hungover lifties at 7:30 in the morning. (It's still shabby.) Proof of the power of the deadline effect: it got three dozen college-age kids out of bed before sunrise.

People drifted in one by one, and John Young, the head of lift operations, gave them their assignments. He congratulated the crew on the saves they made yesterday—"Wow moments, like catching kids falling out of chairs"—and told everyone to avoid tracking dirt onto the snow, an early-season hazard. "Coffee stains can lead to rapid melting," he said, "and snow is a fragile resource." He also offered up a novel description of Donation Day, which he called "our hard/soft opening, our mid, uh, viscous opening." He squinted at his own strange metaphor.

Young was older than most of his employees by about a decade, and he acted as a sort of surrogate father to many of them. He encouraged everyone to come to the staff dinner at the local high school. "This might be your first Thanksgiving away from home," he said, and there was no shame in missing your family.

He closed the meeting by wishing everyone a Happy Thanksgiving: "I'm thankful to be with all of you." The lifties paired off and went to their assigned chairs, and I joined them out on the mountain. Already things looked tidier, more fin-ished. Engler and Deines had been out all night grooming again, and the ski patrol had put up more ropes and signs to steer guests away from tricky spots in the terrain. Plus it had started to snow, the first time since I arrived, putting what Jen-sen called a fresh coat of paint on everything.

The resort had opened seven of its twelve restaurants. During lunch at Gorrono Ranch, there was a fire burning in the fireplace and a small but happy-looking group of guests eat-ing ski-lodge staples like chili and burgers. (Some of the nicer restaurants on the mountain go well beyond that, with tasting menus and extensive wine lists. The resort brings in $2.25 mil-lion in revenue each year from wine sales alone.)

Near the bottom of chair 1, I spotted Scott Pittenger, on skis instead of a snowmobile for once. Jensen sees a bright fu-ture for Pittenger. Both men had started in operations, and Jen-sen was a believer that a CEO who had worked out on the hill made for a better leader. If Pittenger ended up running every-thing at Telluride, it would be years in the future. In the mean-time, he had a mountain to build. The lifts were running, but everyone knew the real deadline was Christmas. Already the news that the mountain was open on Thanksgiving had led to a 14 percent surge in season pass sales. One person in the sales office told me the phones had gone crazy after they announced they would be opening on time this year.

Pittenger and I boarded chair 1 and rode the lift to the top together. We talked about that pesky hydraulic-oil leak and the need to get that covered up. I asked him how many days he was going to take off when the baby was born, and he said, "Not many." After a while we just looked down in silence at Mead-ows, and the handiwork of the past three weeks. There was no doubt that when the crowds came, they would be ready. They were ready now.

4

Focusing Your Mission:
John Delaney's
Presidential Campaign

John Delaney wanted to run for president, which meant that he would have to write a book. That wasn't always the case for a would-be commander in chief—it's hard to imagine LBJ sitting down in front of the typewriter every day—but for a Democrat running after Obama and *The Audacity of Hope*, it was a requirement. To tell his story, to maybe get some press, but also just because it was *what presidential candidates did*, he needed to publish something.

Delaney was the first person to officially declare his candidacy for 2020, which he did in the summer of 2017, more than a year before Bernie Sanders or Elizabeth Warren or Joe Biden got in the race. The book followed shortly after that, once he found a publisher willing to rush something into print. "It was the hardest thing I ever did, writing that book," Delaney told me.

Harder than the campaign itself, which took him to all ninety-nine of Iowa's counties over thirty grueling months.

He started by reviewing all the op-eds he'd ever written, many of them published while he was a congressman representing Maryland's Sixth Congressional District, which stretches from the DC exurbs to the westernmost reaches of the state. He wove those columns together into a twenty-page outline for his book, which he sent to his editor. It was basically a wish list of every policy he had ever championed in Congress, together with an argument for why the country would be better off if these proposals were enshrined in law.

Not long afterward, Delaney got a call from his editor, asking if they could meet for lunch in DC. At the restaurant, the editor was blunt: "This is going to be a terrible book," he said. "Why?" Delaney asked. "Because no one cares about any of this stuff." It was too dense, too wonkish—where were the stories, the vignettes from his childhood, anything to bring this white paper disguised as an autobiography to life? "This is what we're going to do," his editor said. "We're going to have someone come down and interview you for a couple days, just about you and your family and your life and all that stuff. Then we're going to talk about what comes after that."

After the interviews, Delaney had another meeting with his publisher, who had the transcript of those sessions in front of him. "They literally took a red pen and they circled stories," said Delaney. "They're like, okay, you're going to have this story in your book, this story in your book, this story in your book."

One of those anecdotes became the prologue. In it, Delaney talks about his grandfather, Albert, who immigrated to the United States as a teenager, in 1923. A childhood accident had left him without a left arm, and he was detained at Ellis Island—immigrants not considered able-bodied were often deported. At his physical to determine whether he was healthy enough to enter the United States, Delaney wrote, Albert "watched nervously as the official who would decide his fate walked into the room. When he did, young Albert noticed something that stunned him. He could hardly believe his eyes, but the man hearing his case had only one arm."

Not only had Delaney not included his grandfather's arrival at Ellis Island in his first draft of the book—he had never told that story in public at all, even though it had a tidy moral that perfectly supported Delaney's pro-immigrant policy prescriptions. Once the publisher had extracted several anecdotes like this from him, they became the backbone for the book: for every dense policy proposal, there was a snapshot from Delaney's life that supported it. In May 2018, the candidate published *The Right Answer: How We Can Unify Our Divided Nation*. There was a year and a half to go before the first voters got to cast their ballots for the Democratic nomination.

So far we've looked at goals that are clear-cut: opening a restaurant, shipping the lilies, putting snow on the mountain. But what happens if you are faced with a task of such complexity that you don't know where to get started? In situations like that, our gut instincts often fail us: we are poor prioritizers and end up accomplishing trivial goals but make a mess of the consequential ones. Thankfully, to paraphrase Samuel Johnson, a good deadline concentrates the mind wonderfully.

Running for president is a complicated business. To win, you have to do countless things right. But before that, you have to learn how to stay in the race. Anyone reading this will know that John Delaney did not become president in 2020. He didn't even win a single Democratic delegate in any caucus or primary. But while his campaign is now a footnote in the story of that election, it is also a powerful lesson in using a deadline to manage complexity—to stay focused on the most essential goals and ignore everything else.

In February 2019, the Democratic National Committee announced the qualification rules for its first presidential debate, which would take place in June of that year, in Miami. Delaney had been campaigning with his eye on the Iowa caucuses in February 2020, but suddenly he had a much more immediate aim: qualify for the debate. There were many roads to the White House, but none of them bypassed that stage in Florida.

The debate rules were new for this election, the DNC's response to accusations that they had tilted the playing field against anyone not named Hillary Clinton in 2016. There would be more debates, and they would start earlier. More campaigns would have a chance to qualify, too: to earn a spot, a candidate would need to be the first choice of at least 1 percent of those surveyed in three separate polls or raise money from 65,000 separate donors in twenty states. A candidate like Bernie Sanders, who had broad support from the grass roots in 2016, would sail through under the new criteria. But it created an unprecedented test for dark-horse candidates like Delaney.

When I spoke with Delaney's campaign manager, John Davis, he was frank about how much the DNC rules had taken him by surprise: "We started the year with a goal of how do you win Iowa? How do you win New Hampshire? In February we found out the rules, and there was a new contest that you had to win first." What had started as a marathon had become a sprint. Rather than slowly building name recognition, which could later translate into support, Delaney needed people—or 1 percent of them, at least—to decide that he was their first-choice candidate right now.

What I saw when I followed the campaign in the spring of 2019 was an organization remaking itself on the fly. "We had the time and the ability to build an infrastructure to be able to pivot, to focus on ensuring that we got John to the debate stage," Davis said. Everything in their plan that helped them meet the June debate deadline they kept; everything else they pushed to the side. One early casualty: a planned bus tour that would take Delaney to all fifty states. That was a fine idea for a candidate hoping to slowly build momentum for an entire year. But if Delaney wanted to get those three qualifying polls, he would have to narrow his approach.

The DNC rules counted both national polls and those conducted in the "early states": Iowa, New Hampshire, South Carolina, and Nevada. Delaney had been in Iowa for more than a year, so that's where he focused most of his attention. "Our highest probability of getting the polls is in Iowa," he told me, "because that's where we've really been campaigning." This new deadline could even be helpful, by bringing extra urgency to the events he hosted in the state. Delaney would still visit New Hampshire occasionally and try to book time on talk shows in New York and DC just in case they could pick up an extra poll that way, but that was a hedge rather than a strategy. So good-bye bus tour, good-bye South Carolina and Nevada. Iowa was going to be their ticket.

The debate itself would take care of the rest: it would be the first time people in the rest of the country, a great moldable mass of undecided voters, paid attention to the race. If Delaney could turn heads there, prove that his policies were the smartest and, oh yeah, he was the best guy to take on Donald Trump, then the supporters and donations would follow. First, get through the choke point of the debate; the presidency was waiting patiently on the other side.

On March 15, 2019, Delaney was in Madrid, Iowa, a town of about twenty-five hundred people thirty miles northwest of Des Moines. Because the candidate didn't have the celebrity of, say, Joe Biden and Bernie Sanders to draw in a crowd, he picked his stops by asking each county's local chapter of the Democratic Party if they would be willing to host him for a talk, with the attendees drawn from the party's list of contacts.

In Madrid, which unlike the city in Spain is pronounced with a stress on the first syllable, Delaney was speaking at a local senior center next to a VFW and a few boarded-up storefronts. It was 3:30 in the afternoon on a Friday, but still about forty people showed up, mostly elderly, all white. When Delaney entered the room, there was a little stir. "Here he comes!" someone said, and the crowd started to applaud.

Delaney was wearing gray slacks, a blue blazer, and brown loafers. He looked like the judge for a kennel club, perhaps in the sporting group. Although Delaney had been campaigning for more than a year, this was his first visit to Madrid, so he tilted his stump speech toward his bio. "Let me introduce myself," he said, before giving the two-minute version of his life. He was born in New Jersey, the son of an electrician. His father was a union man, and Delaney credited the International Brotherhood of Electrical Workers with getting him a good education and setting him on the path to success. He became an entrepreneur, the founder of two companies that provided loans to small to medium-sized businesses, "the youngest CEO to ring the opening bell at the New York Stock Exchange." He ran for Congress in 2012, represented Maryland for three terms, then retired to focus full-time on running for president. He was a millionaire many times over, though he didn't mention that.

The man who didn't think his grandfather's story was worth telling was . . . a little stilted on the stump. Someone had obviously told him to smile whenever possible, which often made his expression, despite the chipmunk cheeks and toothy grin, seem a little pained and a little forced. He presented a clear contrast to President Trump: most at ease talking policy details and stats, uncomfortable talking about himself. At fifty-six, he was also almost twenty years younger than Trump, extremely fit, and almost completely bald. This last attribute he used as a rare punch line in his speech: "I'm very different than the current occupant of the White House," he said, "and it's not just the hairline." But even that moment turned immediately earnest: "I promise," he said, "to always tell you the truth."

The lines attacking Trump—"the divider in chief"—got the most reliably positive response. The response was decidedly more muted when Delaney pushed the core of his message: a promise to return a spirit of compromise to Washington. In his first one hundred days, he said, he would push forward only bipartisan legislation: "I'm going to be the president that shows you we can actually *do* things again." We need a coalition of voters to govern, he said. Moderates, independents, disaffected Republicans. He cited the title of his book, which came from a speech from John F. Kennedy: "Let us not seek the Republican answer or the Democratic answer, but the right answer."

These were applause lines, but the people weren't clapping. At this campaign stop at least, the voters were looking for someone to fight the Republicans, not collaborate with them. Later I asked Delaney whether he noticed that he lost the crowd when he started talking about compromising with the GOP. "When I go into a room and say, 'Listen, I was ranked the third most bipartisan member of the Congress,'" he said, "I think a lot of people like that. Not everyone does. I can see some people smirking."

That core message of bipartisanship tended to over-shadow even Delaney's most progressive policy ideas: a universal government-run health-care program that was closer to Medicare for All than Obamacare, universal pre-K, massive infrastructure spending, free community college. In this race, Delaney was a centrist, but the center had shifted left. His gamble, that a combination of moderate messaging and left-leaning policies was the best fit for the moment, seemed a little shaky in Madrid, but there were a lot of counties out there.

It was an hour of driving and all right angles to the next campaign stop, a potluck dinner at the public library in Churdan. Madrid was small, but Churdan was tiny: 386 people, according to the last census. Main street, which was called Sand Street, was one strip with a restaurant, a library, the fire station, and an insurance salesman, ending in a grain elevator.

To figure out why Delaney was in Madrid and Churdan while candidates like Beto O'Rourke were talking to huge crowds in cities like Des Moines and Davenport, it helps to understand a bit more about the debate criteria. What did it mean to get 1 percent in a poll? If a survey of Iowans reached 1,000 people, 400 of whom said they were likely to vote in the Democratic caucus, then Delaney would need four of them to say they supported him. That didn't sound like a lot, but to make it happen involved an enormous amount of legwork. No one knew who might get polled, so he had to try to reach voters everywhere in the state and keep them in his camp as long as possible. Voters in Des Moines would have a chance to meet all of the candidates multiple times. In the smaller towns, John Delaney had a better chance of lodging in the memory. "I told my kids a presidential candidate was coming to Madrid," a schoolteacher there told me, "and they said, Why?"

At Churdan, Delaney walked through the library, past racks and racks of children's books, to get to a back room, where he would answer questions and serve soup to the crowd. There was a greater mix of ages here—some parents brought their children and there were three twenty-somethings—but it was still mostly older folks and all white.

The man meant to introduce Delaney, Mike Minnehan, wasn't there: he was stuck on his farm, where one of his cows was about to give birth. So the honor went to a voluble woman named Chris Henning, chair of the Greene County Democrats. Henning said it was appropriate that Delaney was here to serve soup, "because you're looking to be elected to serve all of us." When she noted that he had been to Iowa twenty-five times and visited all ninety-nine counties, people nodded approvingly.

Delaney launched into his stump speech, this time by talking up his Irish heritage and how touching it was to see the St. Patrick's Day decorations in the library. He was just getting to the line about Trump being the divider in chief when Mike Minnehan walked in. That's Mike, someone told Delaney. "Hello, Mike. How'd it go?" Delaney asked. "Got a calf!" Mike said. The room burst into applause.

After the speech, Chris Henning auctioned off a copy of *Born to Run* that had been signed by Delaney. Bruce Springsteen, Henning explained, was the candidate's favorite musician. It was hard to imagine the person who was (1) a Springsteen fan, (2) didn't own *Born to Run*, (3) wanted it in CD form, and (4) wanted it signed by Delaney. But it ended up going for $50, to one of the organizers of the event. Delaney made a little political lesson out of it, about how Bruce always sticks up for the little guy who is struggling.

Delaney opened the floor to questions, and one of the first ones got right to the heart of the matter: "You've been to Iowa twenty-five times. What can we do to raise your profile and make sure you break out nationally?" It was a refrain that came up a lot when I was with Delaney: Why don't people know who you are? The answer, and hope, was that by meeting enough people in towns like Churdan, he'd be thrust onto the national stage, almost literally.

At that point he'd gotten one qualifying poll, the March 9 CNN/Des Moines Register poll, in which 1 percent of those surveyed picked him as their favorite candidate. It was a good start and seemed to prove out Delaney's new strategy. Stick with

Iowa, especially since much of the early polling would take place there anyway, and the benefits would be twofold: he would lay the groundwork for the eventual caucus, and he would qualify for the debate. But he still needed two more polls to go his way.

The rest of the questions were an idiosyncratic mix of issues and grievances: he was asked about school vouchers (against), dismantling the military-industrial complex ("we should have a debate on that"), and a $15 minimum wage (in favor, but gradually). He was good at disagreeing with the audience without seeming disagreeable. A sixtyish woman announced that she was not going to vote for anyone older than she was: "How can a candidate like you politely say, 'You're just an old codger! Go home! Play with your grandkids!'" Delaney declined to take the open shot at Biden, Sanders, or Warren.

The candidate wrapped up by saying, "Thank you all for tolerating me." The crowd started to applaud, but he cut them off to add, "I forgot to say: I would love your support."

Delaney's strategy depended on his ability to effectively focus his campaign on the narrow goals the DNC had set out. He was not alone: effectively meeting a deadline often involves exactly this kind of paring away of obligations to get the job done. To do so, however, requires pushing back against our flawed instincts for prioritization.

Shortly before I went to Iowa, I spoke with Meng Zhu, an associate professor of marketing at Johns Hopkins University. Zhu and two colleagues had published a paper called "The Mere Urgency Effect," which outlined one prominent way that people tend to screw up their priorities. In an experiment, Zhu had asked students to perform a simple task: write five short product reviews. In the control group, they could choose between two different rewards for their work—three Hershey's

Kisses or five Hershey's Kisses. Another group would have the same choice, but Zhu imposed a sense of urgency on the smaller reward. To get three Hershey's Kisses, they would have to finish the experiment within ten minutes. To get five, they would have a full twenty-four hours.

Almost all of the control group chose the larger reward. But when the smaller award was attached to a ten-minute deadline, more than 30 percent of the students decided to settle for three Hershey's Kisses. This was the mere urgency effect: "People behave as if pursuing urgent tasks has its own appeal, beyond their objective consequences," Zhu wrote.

There seems to be a natural inclination to pay more attention to time than to outcomes, even when this behavior can hurt us. We might, for example, postpone our annual physical to go to a limited-time annual sale at a store, even though the importance of the former far outweighs the latter. We attach what the economist George Akerlof calls "undue salience" to the sale, just because it's about to end.

Zhu found evidence that reminding people of the final payoffs—what she called "outcome salience"—before they made their choice diminished the mere urgency effect. In other words, we have to be forced to ignore urgent but unimportant things in order to get our priorities straight. For Delaney, this would mean keeping the final goal in mind at all times: get those three polls. All other activities, no matter how urgent they might appear, should be delayed.

Thankfully, the DNC deadline itself helped push him in that direction. You can see the deadline's impact by looking at Delaney's schedule before and after February 14, when the DNC rules were announced. In January, he made campaign visits to Michigan and Illinois, two states with no active polling at the time. In early February, he went to North Carolina. And then, for all of March, all of April, all of May, it was Iowa, New

Hampshire, Iowa, New Hampshire. That was the sign of a campaign making decisions based on outcome salience.

John Davis had described the change in their strategy as a "pivot," and the tech-world language was no accident. Although it is a cliché to refer to an organization as "like a startup," it is undoubtedly true of an outfit like Delaney's. Juggernaut campaigns like (in a different race) Jeb Bush's had trouble adjusting to the facts on the ground. Small operations like Delaney's could take the new DNC debate rules as they came and change their approach accordingly.

I was reminded of a conversation I had with Travis Montaque, the founder of a startup called Holler, which specializes in visual messaging. (Reply to a text on your iPhone, and a sticker or a GIF created by Holler might pop up on your list of possible responses.) "A startup's superpower is speed," he told me, and that included the ability to adapt.

Holler itself had begun as a news app, and it had built up a small but loyal user base. But when Montaque saw that the company wasn't growing fast enough—and they had only fifty days of funding left—he knew he had to radically change what they were doing. "We can't waste a dollar, a cent," he said, "we have to go solve this problem." He announced to his staff they were going to change from a news app to a messaging app, effective immediately. The users of the existing app would be cut off. "When you have such a tight timeline," he said, "it makes you laser focused on what really matters, and it allows you to make the really tough decisions like, those users don't matter for what we need today." The company now has partnerships with HBO, IKEA, and Venmo, and is growing fast.

On March 16, Delaney gave a speech in Fort Dodge, Iowa, to mark the opening of a new campaign office there, in a narrow storefront in the mostly abandoned downtown. It was his sixth office in the state. About thirty-five people gathered inside. One woman in the crowd told another, approvingly: "I like his message, and he's been to every county in Iowa." She also noted that this was the first campaign office she had ever seen in Fort Dodge.

Delaney told his family's Ellis Island story, which earned a "Wow" from the crowd. The stump speech in general was the best I'd ever hear from him. He warned against the United States "becoming a country of birthright" rather than one of shared values. "A sense of common purpose is the beating heart of this nation."

He talked about how the nation came together during the space race. It all started with an attack, of sorts: the launch of *Sputnik*. ("Remember *Sputnik*?" he asked, which got a laugh.) Twelve years later, by uniting behind a single mission, we had put a man on the moon. Only later did I realize that *Sputnik*, in this metaphor—the frightening thing launched by the Russians that tweeted at us constantly—was Trump.

The first question was another one about Delaney's obscurity. "I like your message," a man said, "but what are you going to do to get on The List?" You could hear the capital letters in his intonation. "I saw The List and you weren't on it." Delaney's response: "I'm going to earn it on the ground here."

He talked about how important Iowa was in selecting the next president. "You ask your questions and figure out what's in our heads. But more importantly, what's in our hearts." The people of Iowa did seem to take their "first in the nation" duties seriously. They came out to meetings like this on a Saturday morning. They asked idiosyncratic questions about every issue you could imagine. And they were willing to entertain the possibility of basically anyone becoming president, whether a frontrunner or an unknown congressman from Maryland.

The opening of a campaign office resembled all the other

stops Delaney made on this trip to Iowa: a speech, some questions, and then he was off to the next venue. The hope, though, was that the presence of a storefront with Delaney signs, brochures, and maybe a campaign staffer inside would be enough to keep the candidate on the minds of at least a few Fort Dodge residents.

So: on to the next stop! These events get repetitive, so I'll focus on one telling exchange with a member of the crowd. Delaney was in the back room of a squat buffet-style restaurant in Mason City, Iowa. He had finished talking to about forty people, and one of the first questions was from a man named Mark Suby, who was old, white, bald, and heavy. If he appeared on CNN labeled as a TRUMP SUPPORTER, you'd say, Yep.

His question—actually, it was more of a comment—seemed to surprise Delaney. "You can't work with Republicans," he began. Instead, we needed to "purge" the government of the GOP. (Delaney winced.) The best thing that had happened lately were all the "new ladies in Congress" who had been elected in 2018, an apparent reference to progressive congresswomen like Alexandria Ocasio-Cortez and Rashida Tlaib. What we don't need, Suby said, is another corporate Democrat running for president.

This was it: the fundamental fracture in the 2020 Democratic primaries. There were those, like Delaney, who thought the Democrats needed a better version of Hillary Clinton to win, and there were those, like Suby, who thought they needed a radical break with the past, whether that was Bernie Sanders or Elizabeth Warren or someone entirely new.

Delaney's response was measured, though you could tell he was put on edge by Suby's forcefulness. "The United States is a centrist nation," he said, and "every single great thing we've done as a country has been bipartisan." Social Security and Medicare, he said, were bipartisan.

Suby would have none of it. It was the right moment for socialism, he said, since capitalism had failed the people so badly.

"If you're going to be a corporate Democrat," he said, "I don't think you'll get the following. I think people are fed up with it."

"I'm not a corporate Democrat," said Delaney. "I *do* believe in the free market—"

"Well, I believe in socialism, and so do the wealthy people. Look what Jeff Bezos was going to do with your tax dollars. They love socialism. Why can't we have a piece of that?"

Delaney looked eager to move on, but a man near the door, a big guy with a gray beard, wearing a blue and white Hawaiian shirt, started talking back to Suby. This was Randy Black, chairman of the Iowa Democratic Wing Ding, one of the biggest fundraisers for the Iowa Democratic party and one of the major campaign events of the summer. The important thing is to unite the party, he said, and save all the capitalism vs. socialism debate for later. Suby said Ocasio-Cortez had the right attitude: fight with everything you've got.

Delaney managed to move to the next question eventually, but the crowd was unsettled by the fighting. Someone said defeating Trump was "crucial," and the whole room seemed to cry out "Oh my God" in agreement.

I talked to Suby after the event, and he told me he spent eleven years as parks superintendent here in Mason City. "I was a Hillary Clinton person last time," he said, but now he was less inclined to seek compromise. American people were slaves to the corporations, he said. We needed to raise the minimum wage now, and any incremental approach was bullshit. He was supporting Bernie, who had been fighting this fight for forty years. His wife kept trying to pull him away, but not without affection.

I asked him if he saw anything he liked in Delaney. "Well," Suby said, "this is his third time in Mason City." He liked that he was doing the hard work on the ground. If Delaney got the nomination, Suby said, he would vote for him, corporate shill or not.

The encounter with Suby seemed to weigh on Delaney's

mind the rest of the day. He said he knew right away that he was in for trouble: "You have that moment when you can kind of tell how they frame the question what their view is." I asked whether he had met a lot of people in Iowa who talked like Suby. Yes, he said, and the ones throwing around the word *socialism* tended to be the loudest voices in the room: "I support the energy and I support the excitement, but I don't support that as the way forward."

At the final campaign event that day, one of the first lines of Delaney's speech was about how he was a proud capitalist. "Socialism in its pure form is the wrong answer," he said. This was at a gathering of donors at the home of Kurt and Paula Meyer, who were considered Democratic kingmakers in northern Iowa. Any candidate who wanted to be taken seriously, one of Delaney's staffers told me, had to spend a night up in their house in the woods near the Minnesota border.

This far north, the snow had survived even the week's rains, and the fields were white all around. It was flat and empty and depopulated, the kind of place where you half expect to find someone frantically burying money in a snowbank.

The Meyers had invited about twenty people to their house to meet Delaney, most of them relatively well-to-do compared to the folks who had turned out for the events at the public library or the buffet restaurant. It should have been a safe space for pro-market Democrats like Delaney, but even here the rift between the moderate and progressive wings of the party was visible. One man said he didn't want the party to nominate a "Republican lite" just because they were scared of Donald Trump. Another asked Delaney about his promise to restore bipartisanship to Washington: "Obama tried it. What can you do better?" Delaney said that reaching across the aisle was the right thing to do.

That night, after the last of the donors left (Delaney gathered a solid handful of checks), Delaney opened a beer and settled down on the Meyerses' couch. He was sleeping over, which was apparently also a Democratic rite of passage. Outside, a staffer on his way back to Des Moines got stuck in the mud, and Delaney had to come to the rescue. He drove his truck, a maroon Dodge pickup with what might be called the Cadillac interior, right up to the other car, put a piece of cardboard between the bumpers and pushed. The next morning, the campaign had posted proudly about the affair on social media. One more reminder, before the pollster called, that Delaney was on the ground in Iowa, working hard.

On St. Patrick's Day, I met Delaney for lunch at Dave's Restaurant in Charles City, Iowa. The candidate was working his way to the northeast corner of the state, to Decorah, where he would host his final event before flying back to Maryland for a few days. The restaurant was full, and the line for the buffet was long. As we waited, two different customers came up to Delaney and thanked him for the message he was bringing to Iowa.

We found a table near the buffet and sat down. Delaney was wearing a green gingham shirt and green sweater in honor of the holiday and looked slightly annoyed to be talking with me but determined to make a go of it.

I asked whether getting on that first debate stage was make-or-break for him. He said he hadn't thought of it explicitly as make-or-break, but "I think it's incredibly important." He was confident he could get there, he said, because of exactly what I'd been witnessing: at that moment, he had the best Iowa ground game of any candidate.

Had he been surprised, I asked, about what people were asking about in his Q&As. "No," he said. "The questions are tied to what the Democrats are talking about," and that included socialism. Also, health insurance came up a lot, he said, because Iowa was botching its Medicaid program.

On the stump he was unapologetic about his centrism, but he admitted to me that he wished he got more credit for some of his progressive stances. He said he was frustrated that the left wing of the party will look at proposals like his and call them "tired old incrementalism." He placed a saltshaker at one end of the table and said: "Let's say this is a bold policy goal such as universal health care, which I share with the left. What does it matter if I want to set a few goalposts along the way" — he grabbed a staffer's phone and placed it in the middle and put his phone a few inches farther along—"if we reach the same end point at the same time?"

I asked, "What if we're in a moment when voters want that bold voice rather than an incrementalist?"

"Then I won't win," he said. "I'm not the loudest voice in the room."

All presidential candidates have to pretend that they are going to win, no matter what their polling numbers are, so it was jarring to hear him state that he might not make it so bluntly. Months later, as the coronavirus pandemic paralyzed the nation, he lamented that American politics seemed to reward qualities he didn't have. "Maybe we will come out of this crisis looking for something different in our political leaders," he wrote on Twitter. "Competence over flash. Forward looking as opposed to living in the moment. Data-driven over talking points. Prudence over pandering."

The drive from Charles City to Decorah was another hour along rectilinear roads. I had asked him earlier whether he and his staff talked policy while they drove around the state. "Noooo," he said. They listened to music; the driver got to pick. When he drove, it was either Springsteen or country.

In Decorah, for once, Delaney wasn't the only entertainment.

It was a St. Patrick's Day fundraising event for the Winneshiek County Democrats, at a storefront event space in the middle of town. There was live music and lots of food, beer, and wine. It was also the biggest crowd I had seen so far, about seventy-five people. They were rowdy and happy. It was a Sunday.

Decorah had a big, stately courthouse, a stone library, a food co-op, and what seemed like a thriving main street (Water Street). This was a part of Iowa that flipped its congressional seat to blue in the 2018 election, though the Republicans won it back in 2020. Before Delaney took the stage, the crowd sang "When Irish Eyes Are Smiling" with remarkable pitch and clarity. Everyone was so united and earnest in its singing it melted your heart. "That's for you," the woman leading the singing said to Delaney.

The song set Delaney off on a more contemplative step than usual. "There's a core beauty to this nation," he said, that no politician could undermine. I was reminded of something John Davis said, about the strategy of sending Delaney to all ninety-nine counties. "You can't fake showing up," he said. "Getting out there and meeting people in their homes, in their diners, their workplaces."

When Delaney left that day, and I couldn't find anyone who would say he was definitely their first choice, I thought of something else Davis told me: "In Iowa they want to kick the tires of everybody, and not just once, but like four times."

Just over two weeks later, Delaney was in New York to address Al Sharpton's National Action Network (NAN), a rare deviation from his Iowa strategy. The campaign had been surprised by getting its second qualifying poll not from Iowa but from a national survey conducted by Fox News. That meant he only needed one more to make it onto the debate stage, and though

Iowa was still his best bet, appearing anywhere that offered him a chance to get on national news broadcasts, even if it was a two-minute hit on Fox Business News, was worth the trouble. "When you don't have high name recognition," Delaney told me, "you go on anything."

The four-day NAN conference drew all the major candidates running for president, and most of the minor ones as well. Joe Biden had not yet entered the race, but Bernie Sanders was here, along with Elizabeth Warren, Pete Buttigieg, Amy Klobuchar, and about a dozen others. The audience was almost all Black, activists from NAN chapters around the country, stuffed into a ballroom at the Sheraton Hotel in Midtown Manhattan. It was as different from the small-town Iowa crowds I saw as you could get. Each day, Sharpton opened the proceedings by chanting "No justice!" And the crowd responded "No peace!" (Or "Know justice!" "Know peace!") "What do we want?" "Justice!" "When do we want it?" "Now!"

The first candidate to speak to the gathering was Beto O'Rourke, who had just entered the race and was drawing crowds in the hundreds in Iowa. The 2020 campaign had seen a few different Democrats seize the media spotlight, and this seemed to be Beto's moment. Sharpton's introduction riffed on Beto's celebrity. "One young man emerged like a rock star, and I'm suspicious of rock stars," he said. But Sharpton gave Beto credit for speaking out in favor of Colin Kaepernick and taking a knee. "I'd never seen a major white candidate for president talk about white privilege," Sharpton said, and so "it's no accident that he's the first of the presidential candidates to come and speak to us."

Later, I asked Delaney whether he wished he could get some of the same attention Beto was getting. He said he was content to let the newcomers have their fifteen minutes: "Muhammad Ali had a famous boxing match with George Foreman where he used a technique called the rope-a-dope. He hung in the fight long enough so that he could win at the end. That's my strategy." He also didn't second-guess his decision to get into the race so early. If he had waited, he couldn't have built out a strong organization in Iowa. "I think if I was getting in now," he said, "considering my low profile, I'd really have no chance."

Beto came onto the stage full of energy, and the room seemed charged by his presence. But the trajectory was the opposite of what I'd seen with Delaney in Iowa. There, the more Delaney spoke, the more the crowd got involved—even if it was just to jump into a debate about socialism. Here, every line of Beto's made the crowd a little bit quieter. After the speech, he hid in a broom closet while reporters mobbed the exit, hoping to shout a question at him.

Delaney's speech was notably different than in Iowa. It was more religious—he talked about Sharpton meeting Saint Peter in heaven and immediately getting in. (He also called Sharpton "a singular figure," which felt a bit like faint praise.) Then the stump speech took over for a bit: the union upbringing, his work in the private sector.

Compared to Beto, Delaney was humble in his address to this audience. "I don't fully understand your problems," he said. "I can never fully comprehend what it means to be Black in the United States of America. And I certainly don't pretend to understand what it means to be Black in the era of Trump." That got an appreciative shout from some in the audience.

After the speech, Sharpton picked up the same thread I had heard in Iowa: With so many candidates in the race, he asked, "how will you distinguish yourself?"

Delaney said he was a problem-solver. He could roll up his sleeves and get things done. By being that person, he was the best person to beat Trump. The audience has gone from listless to politely attentive, which was about the best Delaney could hope for.

He talked to a tiny press gaggle afterward, maybe a fifth the size of Beto's. He was asked why he didn't embrace Medicare for All and dodged a question about Edward Snowden. The Fox News reporter asked, "Can you remain moderate in this race?" The next day, Bernie Sanders and Elizabeth Warren would speak, and the crowd response would make the loudest Beto cheer seem like a murmur. But for now, Delaney had the reporters' attention, and with the right answer, the possibility of making it into a prime-time broadcast. There was time for one more question—actually, it was more of a comment—from a reporter right up front: "Most Americans don't know who you are," he said.

Delaney replied: "Most of my life has been people underestimating me."

On April 11, Monmouth University released the results of its latest poll of Iowa. The twenty-five trips, the ninety-nine counties, the countless potlucks and fundraisers and rallies, had all paid off. Delaney got his final qualifying poll: he would be on the debate stage in Miami. When I saw him a few weeks later, at his office in the DC suburbs, he looked as happy as I'd ever seen him.

He had taken a strategy meant to carry him all the way to the Iowa caucus and reconfigured it quickly, and ruthlessly. By doing everything it took to make it to the debate, Delaney gave himself the only shot he would have to get the Democratic nomination. He told me he was already planning his first two debate-prep sessions. He had two goals: introduce himself and draw contrasts with the other candidates. I asked if he needed to deliver a single, memorable sound bite that night. "I think you have to," he said.

He had laid out his whole vision back in Churdan, shortly

after the DNC announced its new rules: "My strategy is to continue to campaign really hard here in Iowa. The field will get really big, there will be a new candidate coming in every week. The media excitement follows whoever the new candidate is. But that will settle down, and there are going to be some debates in June and July and I think in August and September, people are going to start polling you, after you're all informed. There are going to be some surprises in those polls, and I intend to be one of them."

Delaney, of course, didn't get to be a September surprise. In the debate, he did everything he had to do: he sparred with frontrunners, he made it into the headlines, he established his identity in the race. At the second debate, which Delaney qualified for automatically, the moderators treated him, rather than Joe Biden, as the go-to centrist: they would call on him whenever they wanted someone to rebut the positions of leftist candidates like Sanders and Warren. It was Warren, however, who delivered the most memorable sound bite of the night, and it was aimed at Delaney: "I don't understand why anybody goes to all the trouble of running for president of the United States just to talk about what we really can't do and shouldn't fight for."

It was unfair, perhaps, but it was effective. For the third debate, the candidates needed to meet new polling and fundraising thresholds: 2 percent in the polls and 130,000 donors. Delaney didn't get either one. He was trying for rope-a-dope, but Warren landed a knock-out punch. Delaney stayed in the race for another five months after the September debate. He dropped out shortly before the Iowa caucus, in order to release any voters loyal to him to vote for Biden.

The caucus itself was a disaster, a total failure to plan effectively for a deadline, but that will have to be a story for another book.

5

Revise, Revise, Revise:
Scaled Robotics and
the Public Theater

In a part of Berlin called Alt-Treptow, there is a graffiti-covered brick warehouse that sits on the bank of the River Spree. The neighborhood, which is in the former East, still has the sleepy feel of a backwater, even though it's a short walk away from two of the hippest parts of the city, places where English is spoken as often as German, by an international assortment of artists, writers, and influencers, all looking for a place with cheap rent and vegan options to hide out from the prevailing push and pull of the global economy. The backwater part won't last: already there are luxury towers rising all around, and construction slowed but didn't stop after the coronavirus pandemic hit.

The warehouse itself is evidence of the changes Berlin has seen over the past century. It was built in 1927 as a bus depot; it housed an armory during the Second World War and a refugee camp after it; the Berlin Wall ran within a few dozen feet of its western flank. Now, its concrete floors polished and its skylights refurbished, the building has been renamed Arena Berlin. It serves as a staging ground for art expos, fashion shows, and tech conferences—provided the event is large enough to warrant almost 70,000 square feet of floor space.

On a Tuesday afternoon in December 2019, I banged on one of the building's giant steel doors until a guard opened it. He looked at me skeptically. "TechCrunch?" I asked, and he grudgingly pushed the door open a little wider. Inside, I could see tables and chairs stacked up in preparation for the beginning of a conference the next day. Tomorrow, thousands of engineers, investors, and entrepreneurs—the human fuel for the decades-long tech boom—would be busily networking where 240 German omnibuses once rested. TechCrunch was the name of the publication that had put the whole show, officially called TechCrunch Disrupt Berlin, together.

I passed through Startup Alley, a row of high-top tables with vinyl banners in between them announcing various improbable company names: Joopzy, Joyn, Spurt, Wamo. The startup gold rush, it seemed, was still capable of enticing ambitious young engineers and would-be moguls to devote their lives to whispering promises into the ears of professional investors. The logic hadn't changed: the right idea, molded into the shape of a business plan, could make you rich and change the world, though not necessarily in that order.

One corner of the warehouse had been set off by black drapes that rose to the rafters. This was the main stage, where the central drama of the conference would play out. It was called Startup Battlefield: a competition that pitted the founders of fourteen fledgling companies against one another in an attempt to win over a panel of investors. Each company would have six minutes to present their case for why they were about to change the world (and make a lot of money), followed by six minutes of questions from the judges. A second round, with the field winnowed to just five, would repeat the process, but the question period would last nine minutes. After that, a champion would be crowned and presented with an oversize novelty check for $50,000. For some startups, even appearing on the Battlefield stage was enough to turn their company from a PowerPoint presentation into a viable enterprise.

The crew from TechCrunch was doing a sound check, testing the microphones and the video screens on either side of the stage, in front of about a thousand empty seats. At that moment, a robot came rolling down the aisle. It was yellow like a Tonka truck, with oversize black wheels and a cluster of miniature cameras mounted on its cab. Following closely behind the robot were two pairs of young men. The first pair looked like they were scarcely more than teenagers, and they were staring at the robot with a kind of tickled awe. The second pair were older, in their early thirties, and one of them was holding what looked like a gaming controller in his hand, which he was using to steer the robot.

The one with the controller was Stuart Maggs, CEO of Scaled Robotics, and the man standing next to him was Bharath Sankaran, his cofounder and CTO. The teenagers (actually, they were both twenty-two) were founders of a different company, called Wotch, which didn't come with a cool hunk of hardware: it was a video platform that was meant to compete with YouTube by offering better deals to small-scale "content creators." The two pairs would be going head-to-head tomorrow during Startup Battlefield.

The robot did a quick loop in the back of the auditorium and then came to a stop. "Do you want to give it a try?" Maggs asked one of the Wotch guys, who beamed. He grabbed the controller and gave the little robotic buggy a few stop-and-start zigzags across the floor, asking Sankaran and Maggs a thousand questions about how it worked. Sankaran answered the Wotch guys' questions patiently while the robot skittered about: it was a "reality-capturing device" that could create a three-dimensional map of any room it was in while the cameras recorded photographs of the same space. It was meant to be deployed at construction sites, where it could quickly detect engineering errors. Sankaran was about to go into his full spiel—if you've got a pitch why not use it?—when a woman in her late twenties, wearing a jacket and a wool hat with a pompom on top, entered the room. All four of the founders instantly shut up and looked at her expectantly.

This was Neesha Tambe, who ran Startup Battlefield for TechCrunch. Fourteen rookie entrepreneurs in front of the biggest audience any of them has ever seen, pitching their vision to investors who could change their lives: it was a recipe for flop sweat and onstage meltdowns. Tambe was there to make sure the former was well hidden and the latter didn't happen. She had selected their applications from a pool of more than three hundred, coached them through hours of training sessions, and offered detailed feedback on how they should structure their pitches. She was also, she said, "an unofficial founder therapist."

Tambe walked to the front of the stage. "Companies, come on up," she shouted, and from around the room the rest of the teams participating in the competition materialized. Although the conference organizers, and Tambe in particular, have dedicated themselves to diversifying the pool of participants, all but three of the twenty or so people selected for Berlin were male, and the median age seemed to be about twenty-eight. They shared the unpolished jeans-and-hoodie look typical of Silicon Valley, with slight tweaks reflecting the European flavor of the competition—and most of the competitors: tighter pants, more exotic footwear.

The founders treated Tambe with an uncomplicated obedience that resembled the relationship between a camp counselor and her charges. Her attitude toward them, which was simultaneously upbeat, protective, and exasperated, matched that dynamic. "Let's practice our geospatial skills and get in a circle," she told the group before calling roll. Scaled Robotics? Here. Hawa Dawa? Here. Nyxo, Nodle, Stable, Gmelius, Inovat? Here, here, here, here, here. Wotch? The teenagers smirked. Yeah, here.

"Okay, guys, it's the big stage," Tambe said. "It's time." She explained what they were there to do that day: they would run through the beginning and end of their presentations, just to get them comfortable with the stage, the TED Talk–style headset mic, and to make sure their various slide shows and demos worked properly. "You don't need to do the whole pitch," she said, "just test out the transitions." She went through some basic blocking, which mainly involved telling the teams to address the cameras in the back: the online audience would be an order of magnitude larger than the one in the room. During the Q&A with the judges, Tambe said, turn and face the judges.

By the time the startups actually pitched to the room tomorrow, they would have run through their presentations dozens of times. Ran Ma, the founder of a health-care startup called Siren Care, which won the 2017 Battlefield in Las Vegas, told me she spent hundreds of hours perfecting her pitch with Tambe and the other TechCrunch editors. The stress of preparing for those twelve minutes onstage, she said, "was the best and worst experience of my life. I think I lost a decade off my life span." By the time Ma returned home from Las Vegas, though, she had more than a million dollars lined up from investors. "It's a brutal training ground, but it will catapult your company onto a world stage. You have to have thick skin, be persistent, and get better with every pitch."

Revision based on feedback, indeed, was at the heart of the process—what academics who study management call "effective updating." As part of their applications, the founders had sent in a videotaped product demo, which had been developed into a full pitch and steadily refined in meetings with Tambe over the previous two months. Each meeting ended with a discussion to assess the pitch's strengths and weaknesses. Academics have a name for that, too: sensemaking. Effective updating depends on sensemaking. If you don't know what you're doing wrong, you can't fix it. This approach accorded well with a deadline trick I knew from my work as an editor: get a first draft done and you have the luxury of making it better, pass by pass.

Effective updating was also the logic of the theater, which is a machine built on rehearsals and preview performances. And the competitors at TechCrunch were, in essence, putting on a play. This connection felt even clearer once Tambe led everyone backstage, where she showed the founders where they would get their makeup done. Public speaking leads to a lot of sweat, she said, but a little powder could fix that. Behind her, a half dozen TechCrunch employees were hurrying around setting things up. A separate crew were adjusting levels on a huge audio board and checking the camera feeds on a bank of monitors. The founders took it all in with nervous wonder. Before they started going up to practice their pitches onstage, Tambe had everyone circle around her again: "Put your hand in the middle. 'Battlefield' on three, okay? One, two, three!" Two dozen voices shouted "Battlefield!" into the empty warehouse.

Sankaran and Maggs had a studied nonchalance about them that stood apart from the nervous hustle of the other competitors.

When we met after the sound check, they offered one hint about the source of their cool: they had delivered a version of their pitch to a live audience more than two hundred times. Sankaran, who did the speaking onstage while Maggs worked the software demo, compared it to a stand-up routine. Maggs agreed: "It's been ironed out for literally three years of tweaking and seeing how the audience reacts. Tweaking again, trying out something new."

The company got its start in 2014, after a mutual friend introduced the two founders: Sankaran had been working in a robotics lab at the University of Southern California; Maggs had just finished a graduate program in architecture in Barcelona. Both were dissatisfied, in different ways, with their careers. "I had spent a decade doing all kinds of random robotics projects," Sankaran said. "I'm looking at myself going, 'I've worked on a lot of cool things, but does any of this matter?'" Maggs had reached the same conclusion about architecture. He found the artistic side of the discipline fascinating but ultimately frivolous.

The construction business provided a forum for their twin ambitions: to wield influence across an industry and to tackle a problem that felt suitably urgent. They zeroed in on waste. As much as 20 percent of the cost of a big building project could be eaten up by errors and "rework." (Although, thanks to the planning fallacy, few developers accounted for these overruns ahead of time.) Worldwide, 23 percent of all carbon emissions came from construction. Help builders complete projects more efficiently, and you'd save a lot of money and, yep, change the world.

Sankaran had been interested in artificial intelligence since grade school. He grew up in Muscat, Oman, and every day he came home from school he would watch *Star Trek*. "I wanted to be Spock," he said. "Something about Spock, about logic and being practical about things, was very enduring for me." He said that he still dreamed about space exploration, but he decided that all the big problems of Earth needed to be fixed first.

Oman was a placid place, and almost unfathomably boring for a teenager. Sankaran credited his father, who was the first person in his village in Tamil Nadu to get a college degree, with showing him how much need there still was in the world. "I got a scholarship," Sankaran said, "and he was telling me to go to India to learn how to be street smart. I never understood what that was until I went to India."

Maggs had his eye on architecture from a young age, but he almost didn't make it into his chosen field. At his high school in north London, his guidance counselor asked him to write down what he wanted to do with his life. Maggs, who is dyslexic, wrote down architecture, but he misspelled the word. "The woman looked at me and said, 'Firstly, you spelled it wrong, so that's not a good sign. And secondly, maybe university isn't for everyone. Maybe you should try bricklaying.'"

He bristled at the memory. After graduating, he took a job at a firm in the Netherlands but balked at how unscientific a lot of the decision making was. Once, when he asked a senior member of the firm how he had chosen the size of a building's windows, the answer was simply, "Experience." The architect, Maggs said, "didn't know whether what he was saying was actually true, or the most efficient outcome, or the best solution. It was then that I said, 'Okay, there's got to be a better way,' and I quit that job."

In Sankaran, he found someone as data-driven as he was, though it took them years of talking on the phone before they started working together. Those early conversations were speculative and low-stakes, Sankaran said. "Stuart was talking about inefficiencies in construction, and how robotics and artificial intelligence could help. It was a very academic conversation. It was not about a company or a business." In the meantime, Sankaran stayed in California; Maggs stayed in Barcelona. Finally, in 2014, they agreed to meet, in Paris, a fine city for a founders' romance. Shortly afterward, Sankaran moved to Barcelona, they hired their first employees, and Scaled Robotics was born.

They now had seven people in their Barcelona office, a mix of roboticists, engineers, and mathematicians—Maggs was the only one trained in architecture. The name Scaled Robotics, Sankaran told me, is slightly misleading. They're not really a robotics company; they are a software company. The product they are selling is the detailed three-dimensional map they generate of the construction site, and the data that goes along with it: a list of every wall, column, and beam that can be instantly sorted by size, location, and material. Any deviations from the blueprint are highlighted and can be filtered by urgency, from a duct that's installed a few millimeters off its planned location to a beam that's fatally compromised.

"Everyone gets obsessed with the robot," Maggs said, "but you just have to see it as a data capture device. The robot is fetishized, but we can capture data in other ways."

Sankaran agreed: "The moment you are in awe of some piece of technology, it's not serving its purpose. We want this to become like a screwdriver or a wrench. It's just a fancy hammer."

Why, then, bring the robot to the presentation at all? I asked. Well, they admitted, the TechCrunch organizers had asked them to.

Scaled Robotics wasn't at the conference to attract investors. They already had an exclusive agreement with three firms: PERI, a German scaffolding and concrete formwork company, and two construction-oriented venture-capital funds. Together, they had given the startup three million euros. Sankaran and Maggs would need more money down the road, but for now Battlefield was useful mainly because a lot of their *Star Trek*–watching, data-obsessed peers would be watching, which would make hiring engineers and AI specialists easier down the road.

The lack of a cash crunch at Scaled Robotics ended up helping them. The other teams had a kind of panicky sheen to them, the tell-tale twitchiness of someone in desperate need of money. Sankaran and Maggs benefited from taking the competition seriously but not as a life-or-death matter. "We don't want six minutes to define four years of work," Sankaran said, and that attitude translated into confidence and charisma onstage. By taking pressure off their performance, their performance improved. Depending on what happened at Battlefield, though, Sankaran might not get his wish about those six minutes defining his company. If they lost, yes, everything would continue as before. But if they won, it would change Scaled Robotics forever.

For now, they were poised right at the door to something bigger. The point of a startup is necessarily to grow—to "scale," as the tech world called it, a bit of jargon reflected in the company's own name—and Sankaran and Maggs were doing everything they could to make that happen: attending trade conferences, meeting with investors, picking up new clients. TechCrunch was a part of that same strategy. Even as they competed, however, they were mindful of what they were about to leave behind.

Seven people is intimate enough that the standard business cliché of "we are a family," which both Sankaran and Maggs repeated, could also approach the truth. Sankaran told me that when his father died the year before, he had to leave the business and go to India for weeks: "I went for his funeral, and there was no plan; I was just going. My team stepped in there, Stuart, everyone—they just covered me."

Maggs recounted a conversation he'd had with a member of his team one night, walking home slightly drunk from a Barcelona bar. The employee said he liked coming to work every day, and he was worried that as Scaled Robotics grew, that would no longer be the case. Maggs said he felt the same way: "I don't want things to change. This is one of the best moments of my life. With the money coming in, maybe it will be positive and maybe it won't. I hope it will be positive, and I have the power to try to make it that way, but I totally understand his point of view that you want to preserve those happy things that you have."

At this point, Maggs and Sankaran both seemed to sense that they'd gone too far in underselling their own ambitions. "I know we're making it seem like we don't care about this competition," Maggs said, "but we do."

The first round of Startup Battlefield took place on a gray, drizzly, 40°F day. When I arrived at Arena Berlin, there was a line snaking out of the door, and every few seconds a taxi or Uber arrived to drop off another clutch of wealthy investors, who hurried to the VIP line. The engineers, who mostly arrived by train and bus, waited in the rain.

On the main stage, the director of Station F, a startup incubator in Paris, was talking about the "French tech ecosystem," which was booming. There were more than a thousand companies on her campus. It's gotten so that in Paris, she said, "you see the Eiffel Tower, you see the Louvre, and you see Station F." The audience absorbed this doubtful claim placidly.

Half the seats at the main stage were empty, but next door, at the Extra Crunch stage, the room was so full people were spilling out of the exits. The subject: "What Does It Take to Raise a Series A?" This was typical of the conference: startups were cool, but money was even cooler. Battlefield advertised itself by talking about the number of competitors who got seed or series A funding from investors after walking offstage (a total of $8.9 billion raised), and the number of "exits"—when a company is either acquired by a larger firm or goes public—it has produced (113, so far).

There were some nods to the increasingly insurrectionary attitude about tech in the wider world, in which a company like

Facebook was more likely to be mentioned with disdain rather than awe. A partner of one London-based VC firm stressed to the audience that the companies they support must be either net positive "or at least not net negative" for the world. In some ways, this was no change at all. Facebook, Google, Uber—they had all promised to make the world a better place. But at Tech-Crunch, the emphasis had shifted: show us the problem you are solving. In many ways, the smaller the better.

The competitors in this year's competition reflected that change. Rather than remaking society, the companies promised better sleep, more kids learning to code, and more precise track-ing of air quality. Scaled Robotics wanted to reduce waste, sure, but within a single, unsexy industry, and 20 percent at a time.

As the minutes ticked down to the start of the competi-tion, the seats in front of the main stage began to fill up. Ned Desmond, the COO of TechCrunch, told me that, because a lot of the audience came to the conference specifically to see Bat-tlefield, they took the selection process for the competition ex-tremely seriously. They also made sure every competitor signed on to the process of sensemaking and updating before the final deadline. "Why do we get really good companies?" Desmond asked. "Because the coaching for this event is terrific."

Tambe did at least three training sessions with each com-pany in the month before the conference, and then worked ex-tensively with them during the competition itself to help them fine-tune. Sankaran thought the whole process was revelatory. "You get locked in to a pitch," he said, and all the life goes out of it. Tambe came in with "an outside perspective that breaks the lock, and you realize, 'Holy shit.'"

There were lessons she pressed on everyone: make things simpler, focus on the big picture, be sure to tuck in some hu-manizing details from your personal life. But the advice could also get quite granular, down to the order of the slides and the intonation of single spoken lines. The training sessions were like the mock services at the Fulton or the daily snowmaking meetings at Telluride: moments to stop, to test, and to improve.

At the beginning of the first round of the competition, a TechCrunch staff writer named Anthony Ha bounded onto the stage. He had a manic energy that somehow also carried an ironic edge, as though he was in on the joke that his enthusiasm was a bit over the top. He talked about the difficulty of getting to this stage, that only 5 percent of applicants were invited into the competition. "They're going to be incredibly nervous," Ha said. "It would be really awesome if every company left the stage feeling like you guys love them."

Ha then invited the judges to join him. Capital was well represented: three VC partners, someone from Goldman Sachs, and the director of Station F, back again, this time in front of a much larger crowd. They would vote at the end of the round to decide who would advance to the finals.

The first competitor was Hawa Dawa, a Munich-based company that promised better tracking of air quality. It was also one of the few startups with a female founder, a woman named Cassi Welling, making the pitch. The company definitely ticks the "net positive" box; they sell their service to shipping companies looking to reduce their emissions footprint. Welling flipped through her slides fluidly. The audience saw only the slideshow itself, but on the stage-facing monitor Welling could see a green countdown clock in the corner, running down from 6:00. She landed at zero just in time, but the question period was a bit more bumpy. One of the judges asked about revenue, and Welling admitted that the company was currently earning something in the "six digits." The poor panelists seemed to deflate at this news, and they used the rest of their questions trying to figure out how Hawa Dawa might make more money. Maybe the shipping companies could pay more! Welling hinted at a few deals with bigger companies in development, which seemed to lift everyone's spirits.

A Finnish startup called Nyxo was up next, and they established a pattern that held true of almost all the other companies: your opening slide should establish the size of the market you were disrupting, ideally in the grandest possible terms. Nyxo was a sleep-aid app, so they talked about the 400 billion euros lost every year due to poor sleep. A startup called Stable was in the agricultural world, so they opened with the total size of the agricultural market—likewise Scaled Robotics and the $17 trillion construction industry. You make Hello Kitty iPhone cases? Great, open with the global trade in electronics last year, or the combined revenue of all parts of the entertainment industry.

Anthony Ha was right that most of the founders would be nervous. There was a virtual conferencing tool called Teooh that allowed users to navigate a video-game-like space while they hold a meeting. The interface looked klutzy to me, but the team got high marks from the judges for inventing something that might cut down on carbon emissions, by saving all those airline flights, and this was months before coronavirus made the necessity of virtual meetings apparent to people the world over. (The company had a launch event on March 18, 2020, during the first wave of the crisis: "Even if you're self-isolating, you don't need to be alone right now. Surround yourself with friends, family, and loved ones around the world.")

A half hour before their presentation, Scaled Robotics was backstage prepping with Neesha Tambe. Sankaran paced near the makeup chair in a blazer and blue jeans, and Maggs, wearing a black Scaled Robotics T-shirt, black jeans, and bright pink sneakers, looked nervously over the control boards. I asked them if they felt ready, and Sankaran nodded but didn't look up.

Nearby, I found a ruddy-cheeked, portly guy in a tweed jacket and jeans. This was Richard Counsell, founder of Stable, who was scheduled to go onstage immediately before Scaled Robotics. I didn't ask him to rehearse his pitch for me, but almost immediately he launched into it: Stable offered insurance on the price of thousands of commodities not covered by the traditional commodities markets—things like mangoes, hazelnuts, and raw milk. Their imagined customers were small-business owners (the example he gave was someone who ran a smoothie stand) and farmers. He also incorporated Tambe's tip about including a personal touch. Counsell was a former currency trader who had studied economics and mathematics at Manchester University, but he introduced himself to me as a farmer. His family, he said, has been raising livestock in the south of England for generations.

His enthusiasm for his subject seemed undiminished by repetition. With references to the $4.8 trillion agriculture industry and struggling Polish farmers trying to make ends meet, it was also the most undiluted form of "we'll save the world and make massive amounts of money while we do it" that I would see all week. Stable had been up and running for four years already. They had $6 million in the bank, partnerships with Harvard, Liverpool, and the University of Sydney, and a team of twenty-five back at his London headquarters. Counsell was, in short, the biggest fish in the competition.

I asked him how the process for preparing for Battlefield, by far the most public presentation he'd ever done, and with the biggest and deepest-pocketed audience, was different from earlier investor presentations he'd given. He credited Tambe with encouraging him to talk more about the people his company would help rather than spending a lot of time explaining how, say, derivatives markets work. "She knows what she wants," Counsell said, pushing everyone toward "utter clarity of thought." He cut one portion of his presentation because Tambe said it was "literally the most boring slide I've ever seen."

And then, there was Tambe herself, ready to take Counsell to the wings of the stage. "This bit is stressful," he said. "Your brain is fizzing." They walked over to a spot near the stage-left entrance, and Tambe began what she called her pre-show ritual. She started with a breathing exercise, telling Counsell to close his eyes and clear his mind. Counsell obeyed, and the two of them drew in long, deep breaths and slowly let them out. She reminded him to think of the big picture, that Stable was going to help a lot of people, and not to get bogged down in the details. She sent him up onstage.

Tambe changes her pep talk depending on the founder. Some needed mainly to calm down, others needed to be fired up a little bit. She tried to remind everyone what their greatest strengths were.

As Counsell began his presentation, Sankaran and Maggs were getting outfitted with headset mics. Sankaran rehearsed some of his lines, gesturing toward an imaginary audience (or an imaginary camera at the back of the room). Before they went on, Tambe ran them through the same exercises she'd given to Counsell. She had them breathe in and out, slowly. She told them to close their eyes. She murmured something inspirational to them that I couldn't hear. (Later, they told me she reminded them how well they knew the construction business, so they needn't be scared of the question round.) Tambe had them do a "power stance," shoulders back, feet apart, a move that was all the more visible thanks to Maggs's pink sneakers. And then they walked out onto the stage.

Both founders had given presentations before, but they decided that Sankaran would deliver this one, with Maggs running the software demo.

"His code for me was 'Don't be a robot onstage,'" Sankaran said.

Maggs agreed: "The last thing I told him before he went on

stage was, 'For the love of God, please show emotion in your speech.'"

Founders aren't actors, and even the best pitches have a stilted quality to them, seeming to exist somewhere between memorized text and an impassioned appeal. Sankaran did a good job of landing some of the early emotional punches, though: he lamented the "wasteful and inefficient" construction industry. "They use chalk, bits of string" — his voice took on a quaver of disgust — "and Post-it notes to keep track of progress on multi-million-euro projects." He flipped to a slide about one of their earliest clients, a developer with a building in Oslo that had a misplaced steel beam. It was only three centimeters off, but it could have threatened the whole project. And then the savior arrives: onscreen, the robot rolls through a construction site as human laborers work around it.

The most impressive part of the presentation, though, was the real-time demo of the Scaled Robotics software. A three-dimensional map of a construction project was projected behind the judges, color-coded to show problem areas, with orange showing errors. "As you can see, you're standing in a sea of orange," said Sankaran. The audience, which normally contributed a background bed of restless shuffling to any presentation, went quiet during this part. Maggs and Sankaran withheld the robot until the very end of the presentation, when it rolled out in front of the judges.

The two looked exultant when they came offstage, but they had to move out of the way quickly as the judges came through. Anthony Ha led the judges to a corner of the arena, where there was a consulting area set off by drapes. As they did their deliberating, I walked out with Sankaran and Maggs. I told them that the judges seemed engaged by them in a way that they hadn't with most of the other teams. Their questions, too, lacked some of the skepticism I saw with the other startups. As we were talking, a man walked up and handed Maggs his card. He worked for Unity, which produces video-game platforms. He saw a possible partnership in helping to animate construction models. Maggs nodded politely. I could see the math going on in his head: Unity had more than two thousand employees. Would a partnership end up swallowing his little company?

Maggs and Sankaran went back to their hotel to prepare for tomorrow just in case they made it to the next round.

In the spring of 2019, before I went to see the startups onstage in Berlin, I saw a different kind of performance, at the Public Theater in Manhattan, the home of Shakespeare in the Park and the birthplace of *Hamilton*. Originally I thought going behind the scenes of a play might offer more lessons about the importance of a soft open, as an addendum to what I learned at Telluride. Bill Jensen and his staff had talked about the first days with skiers on the mountain as a kind of dress rehearsal, so why not see an actual dress rehearsal, with actors and directors and musicians running around? It was only after I got there that I realized that developing a play, like developing a startup pitch, was an exercise in repetition and sensemaking and revision, organized around a final deadline.

The play was called *We're Only Alive for a Short Amount of Time*, by David Cale, a musical memoir about his fraught childhood and coming-of-age as an artist. How fraught: the climax of the play comes when Cale's father bludgeons his mother to death with a hammer. Cale was sixteen. Most of the performance was a monologue, but moments of extreme pain and joy were often expressed in song.

I had thought I would show up the day before dress rehearsal, get the lay of the land, and then watch what happened until opening night. I quickly learned it was more complicated than that. Final dress rehearsal comes more or less in the middle of the process, and there's nothing final about it. The play could change substantially both before and after that date. Robert Falls, the director of *We're Only Alive* and the artistic director of the Goodman Theatre in Chicago, told me that the breadth of changes could be quite dramatic, especially for a new show: "A scene doesn't work and it needs to be cut, or you're working on a musical and you take a song out. Or maybe you're putting in a new song that was written last night. It could be anything from a single line being written or a new second act."

There are multiple occasions during the run-up to opening night when these changes can happen. There are the first rehearsals, which focus on the actors' performances, followed by tech week, when lighting and sound and all the other technical details of the show are refined. After "teching" is finished, there's the dress rehearsal, followed by previews—the first performances in front of a paying audience, which often go on for weeks. Daily rehearsals continue during this whole process, and sensemaking and updating happen all along the way. Finally, after previews, the show is "frozen" for press previews; there will be no more (major) changes after this point. Opening night is no different from the performances that came before, except there is no rehearsal that day and there's a party afterward.

My first visit to the Public Theater was during day four of rehearsals, and I arrived in the middle of a scene. Cale was practicing the exact gesture he'd use to deliver the news to his brother that their mother is gone and their father is in prison. Both hands on the knees? One knee up on a stool? Standing at the end or staying in imaginary eye contact with the younger brother?

The theater was filled with clutter: tables looming over the seats, computers set up to tweak lighting and sound designs, ladders in the rows. Falls spotted me and yelled out, "We are at the thrilling climax of the play!" Over the next few weeks, he would periodically call attention to me. "Remember, folks, we are on deadline!" he would shout, especially when some minor fumble or delay occurred.

Cale was bald, with a beaklike nose, a slouching build, casually dressed in a flannel. He was born in Luton, England, but his accent has been softened by years spent in America. After a break, he jumped back into the scene with his brother. A hint of music came from backstage, then swelled as Cale moved into the start of a song. I felt myself getting swept up in the narrative and emotional pull of it—but then Falls interrupted and asked if they should cut a line that felt a bit jarring. After a debate, Cale agreed.

A similar sort of fine-tuning occurred during tech week, but with lighting and sound taking priority. "The actors traditionally don't feel much pressure at all" during this period, Oskar Eustis, the creative director of the Public Theater, told me. "For the first time in the process, and the last, they are not the focus of work." Cale's show depended greatly on a series of lighting cues, as a backdrop behind the stage cycled through bold washes of color, each reflecting shifts in Cale's mood onstage. Jennifer Tipton was the lighting designer for this production; Falls described her simply as "a genius." During tech, each "draft" of the lighting design would get a run-through, and then she would revise it. Tipton continued to make subtle changes to the lighting from tech week all the way through to opening night. "Once we went into previews," Falls said, "she continued to work every night and make it better and better and better and better."

I asked Falls if the biggest changes tended to happen before the final dress rehearsal rather than later in the process, and he said that wasn't necessarily the case. "Every play comes with things that you will learn in front of an audience," he said, "which makes the preview process essential. It's become an essential part in the modern theater, where the play gets worked on. That's because the audience changes it. You suddenly, at least in my case, see the play through a different set of eyes." I thought of the questionnaires Jean-Georges Vongerichten distributed at every mock service.

Falls cited the example of *Hello, Dolly!*, which was substantially revised after preview performances in Detroit and Washington, DC, left audiences cold. Carol Channing, who originated the role of Dolly, said that the text changes were so frequent that they had to hide a member of the crew in a barrel onstage to prompt the actors if they forgot their new lines. Eventually, multiple new songs were written to rescue the show, including the now-classic "Before the Parade Passes By," which ends Act I. Channing remembered singing it for the first time in a hotel room at three in the morning, after a marathon writing session by the song's composer. When the director heard it, he grabbed Channing and the composer by the hands and swung them around the room, shouting, "That's it! That's it!" *Hello, Dolly* would become one of the longest-running Broadway musicals of all time.

The changes made to *We're Only Alive* were more modest, but they were ongoing as tech week led into the first previews. One of the last things they worked on was the curtain call. Cale wanted to stay onstage for his final bows, but Falls made the decision to send him offstage and then back on. It was more satisfying, more final that way, he said.

I went to two preview performances, and I could see how the show shifted once the audience was there to respond: it got looser, more sentimental, and funnier—because despite its material, Cale's script is stuffed with humor. The performance space heightened the sense of intimacy: it was a three-quarter-thrust theater, which meant the audience surrounded the stage.

The effect was to efface the distance between performer and audience, and once the connection was made, it was never broken.

The mechanics of working through rehearsals, tech, and previews to arrive at opening day allowed for the maximum amount of revision, with a heavy dose of it aimed at exactly the right target: the audience who would be the final arbiter of whether the show was a success or failure. The audience were the teeth in the soft deadline, and Cale and Falls—and the creators of *Hello, Dolly!*—did exactly what you're supposed to do once you meet a soft deadline: use the extra time to make whatever you're doing even better.

At the end of the last performance I saw, the crowd yelped itself into a burst of applause. Cale left the stage and then returned, as rehearsed, for the curtain. A woman sitting nearby was crying, as the rest of the crowd got to their feet, still clapping.

The Public Theater had tech week and previews; the startups in Berlin had the training sessions with Tambe. In both cases, there was a well-defined moment when revisions could take place, and that, as it turns out, can make all the difference in whether the final product is a hit or a flop. It's not a coincidence that each version of the lighting design was called a draft.

My work as an editor involved a similar process. Each new draft of an article was a moment to pause, reread, diagnose problems, and suggest changes. On some of the most complicated stories I edited, the writer and I would go through ten, fifteen, twenty drafts to get to the final product. Though of course that wasn't truly final, either: after the writer and I had agreed on a version we both liked, another editor would read the story fresh and give his or her comments. Then the art department, the fact-checkers, the copy editors, and the proofreaders would all have their say, and the story would shift, in ways as blatant as a new showstopper and as subtle as a new curtain call, until at last it was ready for the printer.

We didn't use these names at *GQ*, but we were engaged in sensemaking and updating. Successful organizations have mechanisms to ensure effective updating; poorly run ones stick with their original assessment no matter what the evidence shows. Marlys Christianson, a professor at the University of Toronto who studies organizational behavior, wrote about the potential for disaster when workplaces are unable to, in effect, create a fresh draft for themselves.

In "More and Less Effective Updating," published in 2019 in *Administrative Science Quarterly*, she compared the performance of nineteen different emergency-medicine teams during a training exercise. Each group of doctors and nurses was presented with the same scenario: a small boy with a history of asthma was brought to the ER complaining of trouble breathing. The teams were tested on how quickly they could figure out that a vital piece of medical equipment, the bag-valve-mask, was broken, and how effectively they updated their assessment of the situation once they did. If they didn't replace the bag, the boy would stop breathing and go into cardiac arrest.

"The ability of teams to adjust the sense that they have already made is a cornerstone of effectively managing unexpected events," Christianson wrote. The goal of the experiment was to see how the time pressure brought on by the boy's worsening condition affected the team's ability to do just that. Her hypothesis was that "dysfunctional momentum" could prevent teams from "redirecting ongoing action if sensemaking is not periodically interrupted and reevaluated."

Of the nineteen teams in the study, eight noticed the broken bag quickly and fixed the problem. Of the remaining eleven teams, six were able to pause and update their assessment, sometimes running through multiple different explanations for why the boy wasn't getting any air, before arriving at the solution. Five never did. "Trajectory management—how teams balanced the work of making sense again with the work of patient care—emerged as a key factor that contributed to effective updating, particularly when updating took place over an extended period of time," Christianson wrote.

The teams that doggedly kept reassessing their situation and changing their actions accordingly did well. The ones that stopped looking for new cues from the patient once they got stuck did not. For both of them, there was plenty to keep them busy just in the normal run of patient care: setting up an IV, pushing medications, drawing blood, intubating the patient's airway, performing CPR once he went into cardiac arrest. Finding moments to keep updating was not easy, but the best teams did.

At TechCrunch, moments for revision were built into the schedule: with the first draft sent in to the competition, with each of the training sessions with Tambe, at sound check, at final run-through, in the final pep talk before the teams went onstage. At the Public Theater, the process was even more formalized: the director was expected to give notes at every rehearsal, every tech day, every preview. These were ways of pushing back against momentum, whether dysfunctional or not, to ensure that there was always time to revise.

One of the failure cases that Christianson studied was called Team Oscar. She wrote about how quickly things fell apart once they stopped updating their assessment of the patient's needs: "The patient's condition continued to worsen. Several team members suggested an obstructed tube as a plausible explanation, forgetting that the patient had been extubated midway through the simulation and therefore had no tube in place to be obstructed. At this point, the team was no longer able to generate plausible explanations. They were given a clue by the simulation staff ('What's that mnemonic when you can't ventilate . . .')

as a prompt to help them develop plausible explanations, but despite this clue, the team remained stuck, unable to update effectively, and the simulation staff halted the simulation." If the boy had been a real patient, he would have died.

On the day of the Startup Battlefield finals, Maggs and Sankaran arrived at Arena Berlin wheeling two giant suitcases, which they would use to transport the robot home after the competition. I asked them how they were feeling. "Strong," Maggs said, "but there's still one more step to go."

The night before, they told me, all the founders had gathered for dinner at "some German restaurant" with Neesha Tambe and other conference VIPs. At 9:30, toward the end of the meal, TechCrunch announced the five finalists who would be competing the next day. Or rather, they didn't announce it: an article naming the five was posted on the TechCrunch website while the group was eating—an appropriately tech-y, nonconfrontational way to break the news. I pictured twenty founders eagerly refreshing their phones while trying to make small talk over schnitzel.

Maggs said the dinner was tense, a cutthroat atmosphere leavened by uneasy jokes. "It's all a bit *Lord of the Flies*, isn't it?" he said.

When they found out they'd made it through to the next round, Maggs and Sankaran high-fived but were careful to keep from celebrating too boisterously. They also decided to leave their bottle of wine unfinished so they could get as much rest that night as possible. "If you've lost, then you can go out until one or two or whatever," said Maggs. "Maybe go to the Berghain and have a good time." Scaled Robotics, Hawa Dawa, Gmelius, Inovat, and Stable—none of their founders would go clubbing in Berlin that night.

The final round was at 2:00, and the winner would be announced at the end of the conference, at 4:45. Maggs revealed that he wouldn't be there when the winner was announced: he had to fly to London for a wedding, and his flight would be boarding right when the trophy was awarded. I asked what they would do if they won. Call each other? Sankaran: "Probably a text."

They laughed at their sangfroid, but I pointed out that skipping the extra wine was proof that they were taking Battlefield seriously. Sankaran agreed. Even though they had investors already in place, there were future investors who might be watching. He also called it "a phenomenal recruiting tool." If they won, he said, they would be able to add to their staff: $50,000 was the equivalent of a new hire's full-time salary.

The unfakeable part of their calmness, though, remained. Tambe's process had something to do with it. They had already met her first deadline: the submission date for all entries into the competition. In the weeks that followed, they had revised the pitch with her, eliminating weaker moments and introducing new talking points. These were preview performances, of sorts, with Tambe playing the part of a paying audience. Slides were rearranged and a few sequences, including the anecdote about that particular misplaced beam in Oslo—Scaled Robotics' equivalent to "Before the Parade Passes By"—were written anew. They had even "teched" the performance, on the first day I saw them, in the presence of Tambe.

It was all an answer to the question of what you could do with the time you bought by using the deadline effect, and especially by setting deadlines early, and in multiple stages. If you embraced previews or soft opens or mock services, you could use the extra time to revise. Sankaran said they had embraced that idea early on. "Our philosophy," he said, "is having a plan B for our plan Bs."

The finals of the competition followed the same format as the day before. The big difference would be in the question period, which was now longer than the presentation—a full nine minutes.

For the first time all conference, the seats in front of the main stage were full. A thousand people were there to see the pitches in person, and another ten thousand were watching online. At two o'clock, Anthony Ha came out and warmed up the crowd. He was wearing a suit—a nod to the solemnity of the moment. Ha talked about the instructions given to the judges. They were to assess companies based on their viability first, and then give extra points for social or financial impact. (Make money and change the world.) While he spoke, the Battlefield trophy was placed at center stage. It was a bulky thing, a silver cup perched atop a black block with the names of previous winners engraved on it.

Then Ha invited the judges onstage: four investors—three from VC funds and one from SoftBank, the Japanese investment giant that had recently made news for the extraordinary size of its losses after investing in WeWork—along with Mike Butcher, TechCrunch's editor-at-large, who would act as a sort of jury foreman. The judges had matching green notebooks, which they used in a slightly showy way to make notes during the presentations.

A company called Gmelius went first, pitching a productivity tool that made it easier for email, Slack, and other organizational tools to communicate with one another. Butcher jumped right in with the fatal question: Wouldn't Gmelius revive email, just when we're all trying to cut down on email bloat? (Butcher called the prospect "strange and problematic.") The representative from Gmelius was unflappable: "We believe the email inbox is not going anywhere." Probably true, but also too fatalistic a view of human nature to sit well with the Battlefield judges.

Hawa Dawa was up next. Welling's pitch was smoother this time, but there was a bit of an eating-your-vegetables feel to the proceedings. The judges seemed bored. Butcher perked up briefly when Welling told him they had an NDA with a shipping company but she could tell him more details backstage. "Ooh, interesting," he said. Welling shook all the judges' hands on her way offstage. "Shaking hands is not required," Ha said.

If Hawa Dawa was all about virtue, Inovat was more an admission that vice, in the form of Louis Vuitton bags and tax avoiders, will always be with us. The two founders of Inovat, a Russian and a Ukrainian based in London, promised to streamline the process of getting your VAT refund at the airport. (It was apparently a multi-billion-dollar business.) The presentation was timed down to the second; the final word hit right at zero. The judges were grinning at the end: finally, something useful but trivial. They also seemed peculiarly well versed in avoiding VAT on luxury purchases, naming a few competitors already working in the field during the question time. Butcher the butcher, however, dispensed with Inovat with a yawn: "It's quite an obvious thing to do," he said. Inovat's founders didn't shake any hands.

Sankaran and Maggs took the stage. The judges seemed disengaged at first: the slide about the $17 trillion construction industry seemed like boilerplate, and Sankaran didn't make clear, exactly, that the misplaced beam in Oslo was discovered by Scaled Robotics. But then, when the demo started up, the judges sat up straighter. Their software had the virtue of seeming both powerful and straightforward. The judges started scribbling notes. Sankaran even made sure to hit the environmental note in a way he hadn't before, emphasizing that errors in construction lead to greater waste and pollution. The judges nodded. Maggs sent the robot rolling out past their feet.

Butcher got right to the heart of things by asking why they

bother with a robot at all. Wasn't their real product their soft-ware? Sankaran smiled; he couldn't agree more. He said that the robot was particularly good at capturing reality, but they could take data from any source. In jargon: they were "plat-form agnostic." Another judge asked about resistance among builders to their product. Wouldn't they piss off a lot of people by pointing out their shoddy workmanship? Sankaran admit-ted that some contractors might be annoyed, but in general, he believed, people want to know they've done the work right.

The last presentation came from Richard Counsell, from Stable. Like a proper English gent, he opened with a sporting "Guten Tag," before jumping into his pitch. Butcher sat at the edge of his seat. Quite quickly, it began to look like the compe-tition would come down to Stable versus Scaled Robotics. The judges seemed maybe too impressed, though: it wasn't clear they truly understand what Stable did. To some extent, start-ups had to capture the public's imagination in a single slogan, and Stable failed this test. Where it succeeded was in seeming suitably big, moneywise, and suitably world-changing. Counsell bounded off the stage looking happy.

With the last pitch completed, the judges adjourned to their curtained room, while the competitors gathered at a sin-gle long table in front of the audience, below the stage. Before they announced the winner, though, they would be subjected to a conversation with a previous Battlefield runner-up, Matthew Prince, the CEO of Cloudflare, a company that provides a lot of the infrastructural underpinning of the web. It was currently valued at more than five billion dollars.

Prince talked about his own experience at TechCrunch Dis-rupt. He said his company had 1,000 customers when he went onstage and 10,000 when he stepped off. Some of this year's competitors were studying him raptly, laughing nervously at his jokes. Maggs was on his way to the airport. Sankaran was reading an academic paper on his laptop. I could see he'd made a photo of his father his desktop background.

As the time for the announcement grew closer, the founder of Inovat's leg started shaking so violently that Sankaran reached over and started rubbing his shoulder to get him to calm down. Counsell was sweating and fanning himself with his ID badge. And then finally, it was time to award the cup. Butcher came onstage. Rather abruptly he said, "The winner of TechCunch Disru—" before stopping himself and laughing. "I had one job," he said. He had almost messed the announcement up. "The *runner-up* of TechCrunch Disrupt Berlin 2019, ladies and gentlemen, is: Stable!" Counsell nodded his head and ran up to the stage, where he was presented with a bottle of champagne. Sankaran let out a loud whistle.

And then, with barely a pause, they were going straight into the final announcement. The winner of Startup Battlefield 2019 was: Scaled Robotics!

Sankaran smacked the table with both hands, his nonchalance evaporating instantly. He jumped up and ran to the stage, looking dazed and delighted. A bottle of Veuve Clicquot appeared and he lofted it above his head as a shower of confetti exploded above him. Anthony Ha brought out a giant check made out to Scaled Robotics and handed it to Sankaran: $50,000. Butcher called all the competitors up to the stage, and they posed for a photo. In the final photograph of all the competitors, Sankaran was in the back row, barely visible behind the others.

The top two finishers had both come into the competition well prepared: each told me they had given investor presentations dozens of times. But Scaled Robotics carried the day, I would argue, because of the revisions they had made to their standard presentation. They knew they didn't need investors, at least not right away, which took some pressure off them. But that also allowed them to tailor their presentation to a new audience—to possible future employees, which required them to broaden their appeal beyond bottom-line-focused bankers or industry insiders. That proved to be a crucial change. "The presentation went through a lot of versions in the run-up," Maggs said, "testing what works, what doesn't." The final result made a case that even the Butcher couldn't deny.

The path in front of Sankaran and Maggs was now pitched a little steeper: new staff, new investors, maybe even that eventual exit—it would all come quicker. It was a future they faced with some ambivalence. "It will be very difficult to walk away," Sankaran said. "This startup is an extension of your own self. You pour all of your good and bad personality traits in there. You spend literally years crafting this thing. To hand it over to someone else would be really hard."

Sankaran tried to make his way out of the arena, but he kept getting stopped by well-wishers, along with a few potential investors. As politely as he could, he told them to get in touch later—he had a phone call to place to his cofounder. One of the guys from Wotch ran up to him: Should they crack open that bottle of Veuve? Sankaran promised he'd buy a round for everyone, but this bottle he was going to save for his team back in Barcelona.

Finally, he broke free from the crowd and headed for the exit. The last I saw him, he was alone, heading for a taxi, dragging his giant check behind him.

6

Becoming a "Mission-Driven Monster": Best Buy

I never intended to get a job selling TVs at Best Buy. My plan had been to do what I'd done for all the other chapters of this book: find someone inside the company to be my guide during a big deadline—in this case, the store's preparations for Black Friday—and show up with a notebook in my hand. But after an early conversation with a member of the corporation's PR team, the whole operation went dark on me. I made fruitless phone calls, left friendly voicemails, followed up via email. This went on for more than a year. And then:

Hello Christopher,

Thank you for your interest in joining Best Buy! We received your submission for the following position: Customer Experience Specialist, Seasonal - 734928BR.

We are currently reviewing your qualifications in relation to the requirements of this position. Should there be a match, we will contact you with an update regarding your status and next steps in the application process.

Best Regards,
Best Buy Human Resources
Recruiting Team

It was late September, two months before Black Friday itself. Retailers all over the country were starting to hire seasonal workers to handle the holiday rush, and Thanksgiving weekend in particular. The stores would run their best sales of the year, which would bring out millions of shoppers: more than 80 million on Black Friday itself and nearly 40 million the day before (also known as Thanksgiving, until it was annexed by the big-box sales teams). Total sales that weekend would end up reaching $69 billion. It was an enormous logistical challenge: how do you prepare for a day when customer traffic would be an order of magnitude greater than normal?

I was familiar mostly with the catastrophic failures: the stampedes that had injured multiple shoppers; the fights over deeply discounted microwaves and flatscreens; the heart attacks and murders. The totemic Black Friday disaster was the death of a worker at a Walmart in Valley Stream, New York, during a frenzied opening on the morning of November 28, 2008. Jdimytai Damour had been told to stand guard at the entrance to keep back the thousands of shoppers trying to be the first in the store. Shortly before 5:00 a.m., the crowd began chanting "push the doors in." A few minutes later, the first people made it through. "They were jumping over the barricades and breaking down the door," said one witness. "Everyone was screaming." Damour was knocked down and trampled; he was pronounced dead an hour later at a nearby hospital.

In the years since then, retailers had gotten better at crowd control, or they had just gotten lucky, or both. Stampedes became rare, though there were still plenty of fights, especially outside the stores, in the parking lots. Even in the worst days of Black Friday madness, Best Buy was something of an outlier. There was one moment of violence, in 2010, when a shoplifter swung a knife at a marine who was collecting donations for the Toys for Tots program. That incident, however, was more likely an example of "indigenous American berserk," as Philip Roth called it, than a product of Black Friday itself. And if Best Buy was better at managing the day than its rivals, I wanted to know why. Did they use interim deadlines or soft deadlines, like Jean-Georges and Telluride, or was it all in the planning, as it was for Airbus and the lily growers? Whatever they were doing, it was working.

In my application for the seasonal sales associate job, I made it a rule not to lie about anything, but I did leave a few items off my résumé. It included my high school in Atlanta and a selective tour of my work history, making much of the part-time job I had working for a hotel's AV department in college, twenty years earlier. (If Best Buy needed someone to set up a PowerPoint using '90s-era computer and audio tech, I was well qualified.) I also listed the freelance editing I'd done sporadically over the past fifteen years. Not on the list: any full-time job I'd ever had. I had to blow the text up to size 16 to make it fill a single page.

I wasn't dumb enough to think I was likely to get a permanent job at the store, but I was hoping they were desperate enough for temporary help that they wouldn't even look at my scanty qualifications. Even so, I couldn't shake the feeling of ethical dubiousness from the endeavor completely, which was probably the right moral intuition.

Twenty-five minutes after I submitted my application, I got a call from the hiring manager at the Best Buy in Baldwin, New York, which is about an hour by train outside the city. She asked me to tell her a little bit about myself—I said that I was a freelance editor hoping to make some extra money before the holidays—before getting to her real question: was I available to work on Thanksgiving? Best Buy opened at five o'clock that afternoon. I assured her that I could, and she asked if I could come in for an interview. At two o'clock on the following Monday, I did just that.

I won't dwell on the interview, except to say that I thought I performed pretty well. The manager was charming and upbeat, and he seemed to accept my cover story that I was a freelance editor who had seen business slow down recently. (True!) He wanted to know about my availability (open), but seemed most intent on answering two questions: Are you going to steal from us? (No.) And are you going to be a nuisance to your manager? (Probably!) I left the store feeling upbeat, but a few days later I got an email from Best Buy saying, "After careful consideration, we will not be moving forward with your application for this position." I was devastated. Being underqualified for a job, it turned out, was a barrier to getting it.

The next day, I applied for a seasonal job at the Best Buy a few towns over from Baldwin. And then, silence.

———

While I waited for Best Buy, I went to a hiring event at a Target within walking distance of my house in Brooklyn. I still thought Best Buy was likely to have the most organized approach to Black Friday, but Target promised it would be hiring people on the spot if they passed through a screening process.

This interview went a lot quicker. Mainly Target seemed to be checking that I was presentable and enthusiastic and could plausibly steer a customer *toward* rather than away from buying something. I told my interviewer I knew a bit about electronics—just look at my résumé there, under 1999 to 2001—but he said the only openings were in style and beauty. Now, it happened that I knew more than your average dude about style after years working at *GQ*, but I couldn't say this. So instead I told him that style sounded cool and I was definitely eager to learn what I didn't know. And just like that, I was hired.

The next day, Best Buy called me. Could I come in for an interview this week? I reluctantly said yes. It wasn't until I arrived there a few days later that I realized that the store I had applied to was in Green Acres Mall, in Valley Stream. The Walmart where Jdimytai Damour was trampled to death was one parking lot away.

At noon on a cold November day, the area had a forlorn feeling. There was a Target and a TGI Friday's, a Home Depot, and the Walmart where the disaster happened. Blue tarps waved in the wind above a Macy's that was either being torn down or very slowly put back together. I walked across the parking lot, toward a swooping blue façade with a giant yellow Best Buy price tag looming over the door.

The box was indeed big: thousands of square feet for TVs, a big blob in the middle for phones and games, a wing devoted to fridges and appliances, and in the back, a section for laptops, tablets, and computers. The ceilings were high, which gave the place a less claustrophobic feel than Target. Also, there were almost no customers in the middle of a weekday.

My interview was with the store's general manager, whom I'll call David. (Because none of the employees in Valley Stream knew I was a reporter, I've changed names throughout this chapter.) He was in his mid-thirties, with a weary look on his face, a paunch, curly brown hair. His first question, of course, was about my availability. He also asked why I chose

Best Buy and I mentioned that I'd been into computers my whole life. Also that I wanted a retail job for the season, but it was hard to imagine working in (say) the style section at Target. He nodded.

He then took me through the list of scenarios I might face if I worked at Best Buy: What would I do if I had one hour of work left to do but fifteen minutes left in my shift? What if someone had an online order and it was missing a part? What if a customer insisted she gave me a $50 bill and I thought she had given me a $20? He also asked me what I'd do if I caught an employee stealing something. I'd report him to my manager, of course, I said. And if you were the manager, what would you do? Fire them. And would you report him to the police? Here I paused. I knew that the "right" answer was zero tolerance, but I couldn't imagine that, if I were actually a Best Buy manager, I'd want to send a minimum-wage-earning kid to jail just for nicking some gaming controllers. David looked at me warily. Call the cops, I said.

David skipped a bunch of questions and then got to the last page, where the manager was supposed to score my performance. He circled all 4s on a 1-to-5 scale and then asked when I could start. Something perverse in me made me want to press my luck. "Cards on the table," I said. "I've got another job offer." David pursed his lips. "It's in the style section at Target. And while I'd rather work here, they're offering me $15.50. I'd want to at least beat that." He hesitated a microsecond before agreeing to $16 an hour: "Sure, we can do that. We don't like those guys over there." At Target, he meant. Only later did I realize how accidentally gutsy this was: $15 was minimum wage in New York City, where my Target offer was from, but in Nassau County it was $12 an hour.

On the way out, we talked about Black Friday, now just three weeks away. He'd done fifteen of them with Best Buy.

They were expecting 5,000 to 7,000 customers, compared with a normal day of 500 or so. I told him that was part of why I wanted to get this job: it seemed exciting to be in the thick of that mad rush. "Oh, it's exciting," he said, "and crazy." With that, he shook my hand, and I was officially a Best Buy employee. I called Target to tell them the bad news.

They were out of the signature blue Best Buy polos, so I was given a black one instead. Technically the shirt was meant for someone working in the back of the store, in inventory, but customers didn't seem to notice the difference, as long as I was wearing my yellow name tag. I met the store manager, Anthony, who served directly under David. He was compact and wiry, with an exquisitely trimmed, close-cropped beard. He told me he had been at Best Buy for six years, became a manager at twenty years old. He talked up the store's culture of promoting from within: 85 percent of supervisors and 80 percent of general managers were promoted internally. "If you want to be CEO of the company," he said, "you can do that."

During my training, I'd watched an orientation video about the history of the company, back to the original store in St. Paul in the 1960s, when it was called Sound of Music. After a spinoff location was hit by a tornado, in 1981, the resulting sale of distressed inventory led the founder to the idea of radical discounting. One name change and a few barely profitable decades later, and Best Buy arrived at 2012, when it nearly went out of business in the face of competition from Amazon. That was the year that Hubert Joly, a businessman born in Nancy, France, arrived as CEO with the mission of turning the company around. The first thing he did was introduce a price-matching policy, to stop Amazon from always undercutting them. And he played up the things—like customer service and tech support, in the form of the Geek Squad—that might make someone still want to go to a physical store.

Joly was, in some distant sense, my boss, so I'm hesitant to praise him too much, but his actions did seem to stabilize the company. As other big-box stores, including those that were making life miserable for the Easter lily farmers, suffered during the "retail apocalypse" that was closing malls around the country in 2019 and 2020, Best Buy was holding on to its customers; sales had grown in the previous five consecutive years. In 2019, the company had more than 125,000 employees globally and $40 billion in sales. "We're the largest omni-channel consumer electronics retailer in the world!" the orientation video chirped.

I had asked to work in the computer department, which seemed like the one part of the store where I wouldn't be totally lost, but Anthony told me I'd be in home theater instead. TVs. I told Anthony that my television at home was ten years old, and it was a plasma—a type of screen they don't even make anymore. He said it didn't matter: I could learn, and home theater was where they needed the most people on Black Friday. A flatscreen was still the prize most people wanted to take home on the big day.

No one in home theater seemed to know I'd be joining them, but they rolled with it quickly. I met my immediate supervisor, Sid, and Robert, a veteran sales associate whom I would be shadowing on my first day.

Robert, a solidly built guy in his mid-thirties with a Caribbean accent, seemed amused that I was there to watch him work, but he didn't object. He gave me a quick tour of the home-theater section, which took up a few thousand square feet in the right front corner of the store. Home theater covered everything from stereos to HDMI cables to antennae, but the star of the show were the flatscreens. These were separated into three main subsections: the wall of Samsung, the wall of Sony, and the wall of LG. All the other TVs, from the cheapo TCLs to the Toshibas, Vizios, and Sharps, were relegated to the margins. The steady goal of any sales associate working the floor was to steer people from the lower-priced TVs to the Big Three.

With a few exceptions, all the customers I met during my regular shifts came in with the expectation of picking up one of the lowest-priced TVs. But the Big Three were so beautifully arranged, with special high-contrast color-choked videos playing on a loop, that most people spent at least a little bit of time pondering a life in which they could afford one of the higher-end models. The price differences could be dramatic: the most expensive TV in the store, an 82-inch Samsung playing 8K content, which didn't even exist in the real world, was $6,000. The cheapest ones hovered between $100 and $300. They were all much, much better, and bigger, than the TV I had at home.

Robert talked me through the basics of the job: try to push people into higher-end models, try to attach speakers and add-ons to their purchase, try to get them to buy warranties and tech support or sign up for the Best Buy credit card. (Each credit card application, each "app," would get the store $200.) Always be upselling: someone may think they're here for the $249 special they saw, but really they are a future top-of-the-line man-cave mogul ready to be unleashed. The general rule was that any upsell was good. If someone had been pushed up a category but showed resistance to go any further, stop pushing. At one point, Sid walked by and saw a customer holding a mid-range Sony. He started to talk about the drawbacks of that TV, but he shut up once Robert explained that the customer came in looking for a TCL. "That Sony is a great TV," Sid said.

I got to watch only a few sales with Robert before he disappeared. Eventually I found another seasonal employee, Eric, who had two weeks on the job already and was thus vastly more knowledgeable. At one point he paused and gave me a once-over, eyebrows raised. "How much are they paying you?" he asked. Sixteen dollars an hour, I answered. He didn't seem surprised; it was more like I had confirmed a suspicion of his. He was getting $14.25. I figured if there was one good deed I could do while working this job, it would be to get my colleagues a little more money, so I told him he should ask for a raise to $16 and feel free to tell David, the manager, that he knew that I was getting paid that much. He said he would.

After a few hours, I managed to stumble into an actual sale. A guy in his early fifties with a graying goatee was staring a bit distractedly at some of the Samsungs. He told me he had come in to get one of the TCLs, which he had heard were pretty good. I walked him over to the TCLs. These were all crammed in together, which had the effect of making it hard to differentiate one from the other. We squinted at a few of them. He found one that wasn't too expensive, maybe $400, and I agreed that it seemed like a fine TV.

Privately, I had decided that I wasn't going to try to upsell anyone. I was there to observe, not to push people into a TV they couldn't afford. I didn't try to dazzle the customer with technical specs and bang on about the vast differences between a Samsung and a TCL—I couldn't even if I wanted to. I said what I believed, which was that all the TVs were pretty great and after picking the size you wanted, you really couldn't go wrong. But more than once, this led the customer to ask about that higher-end Samsung: like, if there was nothing special about it, why did it have a special spot on the sales floor? And why was the price so much higher? "Well," I would say, "I'm not sure there is much difference." But often, once the customer was looking at a featured TV, it was hard to go back to the rack with the lower-end models.

Anyway, this guy, whose name was Tommy, had just broken

up with his girlfriend, and he was moving out of their apartment. He didn't know whether he wanted to make a big splash in his new bachelor pad or to keep things conservative, as a sign of the seriousness of his new life, his new place. Because I'd basically emptied out my knowledge just by naming the various brands we carried, I said the one other thing I learned in my hour on the job. There was a special on Sony TVs: you got $300 off if you bundled a Sony and one of the higher-end sound-bar speakers. We walked over to the Sony section, and I showed him the sign describing the deal. He seemed happier just to be in Sony-land rather than in mixed-nuts purgatory with the TCLs.

Tommy got on his phone to talk to someone, pacing around nervously. Finally, another associate, Terrell, came to rescue me. He played Tommy a demo on the sound bar, an action-movie soundtrack that pulsed with car crashes and gunshots and whomping bass. Hearing the high-power punch of that audio seemed to solidify something in Tommy's mind and he finally said, "Okay, let's do it."

"Really?" I asked. "Oh, okay! Let's go to the register." When I rang up the transaction, I made sure to punch in Terrell's employee number to give him credit for the sale. They don't work on commission at Best Buy, but the company keeps track of individual sales figures and rewards the best-performing employees with bonuses. Some of my colleagues complained about sale-stealing or employees who would demand to be added to a sale even when their contribution was minimal. I was a newbie, though, so I rarely had a sale that I'd earned on my own, and I was happy to share credit. This seemed to make my presence in home theater, while still annoying because I was basically incompetent, at least somewhat bearable.

Speaking of incompetence: It turned out that the TV I sold Tommy was out of stock. Or maybe there were some in the store somewhere, but no one knew where to get them. I should have just let Tommy go, told him to order it online and get it delivered to his home, but by this point I had spent more than an hour with the guy. I ran back into the storage area, but the TV was nowhere to be found. I searched the store: TVs were stacked up everywhere in preparation for Black Friday, but not the one Tommy wanted.

Terrell tried to help me set it up so Tommy could pick up the TV at another location, but that didn't work either—stores were not releasing their inventory this close to the holiday. Tommy was ready to walk. My first sale was evaporating right at the checkout.

Finally, I asked Tommy if he was willing to place the order now and pick up the TV later that day. The computer said six of these TVs were in stock, so they had to be somewhere. Place the order, some magical elves would find the missing TVs, and the store would email you to pick them up. There was no reason for him to do this. He found a TV he liked and he could surely get the same price online. All the convenience of buying something in person—you get to see it with your eyes and take it home now—had disappeared. Still, out of some misguided sense of loyalty to me, he agreed. Triumphant, shame-faced, exhausted, I rang up the sale: almost a thousand dollars straight to Hubert Joly's bottom line. I had stayed past my official punch-out time by more than an hour.

The home-theater group seemed more macho than most teams. Whenever there was a lull in customer traffic, the guys got together to rehearse a few common themes: music, DJing, making money. I played a particular role in these conversations: the newbie asking questions, which elicited a performance of knowledge and worldly wisdom. It was a lot like being a reporter, it turned out. (I am reminded of something Hubert Joly said in the orientation video: "I would like you to write yourself into the Best Buy story.")

One of the only women on the team was Stephanie, who was a Samsung specialist and thus refused to push a customer toward any TV but the most expensive Samsung. She spent a good hour at the beginning of my second shift walking me through the details of Samsung's offerings: 8K, 4K, QLED, slim array, full array, HDR 32X. At the end, she quizzed me on my knowledge and I was pretty miserable. "You forgot to talk about the quantum dot," she said, and it was true, I had. I also still don't know what that is.

At one point, Terrell and another coworker, Luis, asked me if I was shadowing Stephanie that day. "I guess," I said, though no one had assigned me that role. "You need to get out," they said. "She's bad news." It was true that I never made a sale with Stephanie. The closest we got was a guy who came in looking for a 65-inch TV. He wore sunglasses indoors, had on a Gucci knockoff jacket, and handed us his business card, which promoted his Instagram: @stonerinfo. His account, which had 85,000 followers, consisted of pictures of weed and (weed-related) *Simpsons* memes. He said he was a fashion designer and asked what other jobs I had. I told him this was the only one. He seemed flabbergasted. "But how are you going to make any money?" he asked. I shrugged.

Stoner Info played the high-roller part but seemed unusually price-sensitive. Stephanie suggested he go big with a Samsung, but he kept returning to a mid-tier LG he liked. Ultimately, the whole thing fell apart when Stephanie basically refused to sell him the LG, which she said was inferior, and he didn't go for the Samsung. He asked if prices were going to drop any more and Stephanie said yes, on Black Friday, but you'll have to wait in line with a thousand other people. Black

Friday? "That's the shit you see on the TV where everybody is killing each other," he said. He left without buying anything.

The best experience I had during those early shifts was when I helped a boy and his Spanish-speaking father. The son, who was twelve, translated for us. The father wanted something he could be proud of, he said, something that would last, but their budget was tight. We were standing in the aisle with the cheapest TVs. The father's eye, however, kept wandering over to the Samsungs. He asked for the price. "It's $899," I told him. The son translated; the father nodded. We watched the TV in silence for a while. I offered to show him other options, but the longer he stood there, the less likely it seemed he would be budged. When I rang the TV up, we both got a surprise: it was on sale, a pre–Black Friday special, for $699. "Good," the father said. It was a rare case when my haplessness didn't hurt the customer.

Two weeks before Black Friday, we had an all-staff meeting at 7:00 a.m. to go over how the store would operate on the big day. When I was hired, it was the one date David had me reserve right away: my first shifts might start whenever, but I had to be there for this meeting.

I arrived at 6:45 and already thirty or so people were waiting in the Magnolia Home Theater room, a little store within the store with the highest-end TVs and speakers. There were chairs arranged in rows, and bagels and coffee had been set out. All the TVs in the store were off, which gave the place an almost sedate atmosphere. It took another thirty minutes for everyone to arrive, but eventually the entire staff, seventy seasonal and full-time associates and another twenty supervisors and managers, was gathered in front of the largest Sony in the room.

Anthony stepped up front and addressed the crowd. David wouldn't be leading the meeting that day, he said, because he was "very very sick." He was going to video-conference in, however, for an opening statement—and there he was, looking a bit worn-out but otherwise okay, wearing a Best Buy fleece in the backseat of his car, where he'd gone so he could talk to us without waking up his wife and kid. His illness, it turned out, was shingles, which is often brought on by stress.

He talked up the intensity of Black Friday—"it's the biggest, craziest time of the year"—and the importance of this dry run. Every Best Buy in the country was having a similar meeting at that moment. "If there is one meeting you should pay attention to," he said, "it's this one." So maybe this was one clue to Best Buy's success: they had created the retail equivalent of a restaurant's mock service. I would soon discover, however, that they did much more than that.

David turned things back over to Anthony, who asked the room how many people were working their first Black Friday. More than half the staff raised their hands. "Even those who have worked the holiday before still get the butterflies," he said. "I'm not here to scare you, but it will test you." He then unveiled the strategy the store would use to handle the huge crowds and their abundant, entropic energy. It amounted to nothing less than a total overhaul of how Best Buy did business.

First, the entire sales floor would be divided into five sections, with barriers between them: home theater, computers, gaming, mobile phones, and appliances. Each department had its own "doorbuster" item, so the divisions would immediately serve to break up what would be a giant wave into separate channels. The actual barriers would be made of product boxes. The larger TVs served excellently for this purpose: already I spotted a line of 65-inch TCLs dividing appliances from the mobile-phone section and a row of Toshiba Fire TVs between gaming and home theater. Every section had its own dedicated checkout, with bright pink tape on the floor showing the direction the queue should flow.

Next, customer service and Geek Squad tech support would close from Thanksgiving until the day after Black Friday, and their desks would be turned into regular registers. A single queue, lined by TV boxes and stretching all the way to the back of the store, would feed the main checkout area. That would catch any customer who didn't make it into a department-specific checkout line. There would also be extra security guards on hand, hired from an outside firm. Food for the staff would be catered so no one had to leave for dinner. Employees also no longer got to choose their mealtime but had one assigned to them.

Customers seeking what was anticipated to be that year's most sought-after sale, a 58-inch TV for $199 (marked down from $479), would be diverted outside the store altogether. The first few dozen people in line would be given a ticket, which they would present at the loading dock to pick up their TV. The other item expected to draw a big crowd, an $89 laptop, would be available only in the computer section, which had roped off an extra-long checkout line to deal with the demand.

There was one other innovation that I didn't appreciate until I saw its effect in real time. For Thanksgiving and Black Friday only, the store would no longer track individual employees' sales figures. Every TV, laptop, or Xbox rung up those two days would be credited to the team. Competition among employees might make sense during a normal day—motivating a sale, encouraging upsells, making sure all customers got prompt attention—but on Black Friday, speed was the highest value. This change opened the way for a division of labor that proved more efficient than the usual jockeying for sales: a customer could be handed off, rerouted, and ultimately rung up by different employees with no one worrying about their numbers.

In response to a flood of customers, Best Buy had created a bucket brigade.

Anthony wrapped up his presentation, and we broke up into departments to walk through what we had learned. I was feeling confident, but Sid was more solemn. "Just prepare yourself," he said. "It's not going to be easy."

The reorganization of the sales teams reminded me of something I had read in a book called *Organizations in Action*, by James D. Thompson, which was published in 1967. Thompson was a sociologist, and he became interested in how the structures of businesses affected their performance. One of the attributes he singled out was "interdependence"—that is, the ways in which the various parts of a company or team relied upon one another to operate.

The simplest type of interdependence he called "pooled interdependence": each employee or division contributed to a common goal, but they did not need to coordinate with one another to do their jobs. For the most part, that described business as usual on the floor at Best Buy. Associates work on their own to bring in sales, with numbers tracked individually, and the health of the whole store depended on their combined revenue.

On Black Friday, though, the store switched to what Thompson called "sequential interdependence." Each sale now passed through multiple hands, and no individual got the credit. A sequentially interdependent team was more efficient—like an assembly line, a classic example of the form. This type of interdependence requires more communication among employees, and greater planning on the part of management. Of course, that's exactly what the dry run was for.

The most complicated kind of interdependence is "reciprocal interdependence," in which a single task can pass back and forth multiple times among the employees on a team. There were some examples of reciprocal interdependence at Best Buy, but the most salient example to my mind is (again) a magazine, in which at any given time the copy or art departments might be waiting on me to get something done or I might be waiting on them. In my experience, increasing interdependence correlates to more effective enforcement of deadlines.

Sequential was good enough for Best Buy, though — and it was a fairly radical shift in the way I interacted with my colleagues. It changed the overall dynamic from competition to cooperation. I thought that might have something to do with the lack of sales tracking: without the promise of that reward, even the most cutthroat associate would have no reason to steal a sale. But according to Ruth Wageman, who wrote about interdependence for a collection called *Groups at Work*, it is "task interdependence" rather than "outcome interdependence" that truly motivates cooperative behavior. That is, the bucket-brigade structure forced us to cooperate, whether we wanted to or not.

There was another change I should mention. Whereas on a normal day sales associates would be told to simply bring in as much revenue as possible (or, more likely, wouldn't be given any goal at all), at the start of Black Friday, David read us the specific numbers the store was going for: $725,000 in revenue, 200 credit card applications, 20 new members in the Total Tech Support program.

This sounded a lot like a move borrowed from what's known as goal-setting theory. Gary Latham, who together with Edwin Locke published the best-known book on the subject, summarized the central claim: "We concluded that the most effective goals for increasing performance are those that are specific and difficult." One study of this strategy looked at six logging operations in Oklahoma. The logging companies were having trouble getting their drivers to load their trucks to their full capacity, which translated into extra trips and extra costs. The company managers first tried to get the truck drivers to do better just by telling them to load more logs—to do their best. No change.

They then tried something different: the drivers were now told to load their trucks to 94 percent of their weight limit for every trip. Once the drivers were given a specific, difficult goal, performance improved rapidly. The average load soon went from approximately 60 percent of capacity to 90 percent, and it stabilized there. The move wound up saving the companies nearly a million dollars.

In addition to the changes in interdependence and goal-setting, Best Buy made some tactical moves well before November that improved their ability to manage Black Friday effectively. The Valley Stream store had been steadily building up inventory: in a quiet time, it might get one restocking truck a week. Now it was getting four. The decision to open on Thanksgiving itself, which became the norm among big-box stores shortly after Damour's death, in 2008, was an attempt to distribute the crowds across two days. And of course, the company had hired a bunch of rookies like me to handle the impossible swell of customers and their questions.

Altogether, it was an eye-opening lesson in how even a giant corporation could remake itself to meet the challenge of one particularly important deadline. It's too grandiose to compare the two, but a line from an article about the Apollo program comes to mind. Once President Kennedy had set the deadline to put a man on the moon by the end of the decade, Mike Tolson wrote for the *Houston Chronicle*, "NASA had to be transformed from a multipurpose scientific bureaucracy to a mission-driven monster." Substitute "omni-channel consumer electronics retailer" for "multipurpose scientific bureaucracy," and you've got a fair description of me and my coworkers that November.

The night before Thanksgiving, I woke up at 2:00 a.m. in the middle of a troubled dream: I was desperately trying to price-check a TV, but I couldn't get the scanning gun to work. In fact, I'd been having nightmares about TVs for weeks. I was barely keeping it together during a normal workday; multiplying the number of customers by 10 or 20 seemed like madness.

My shift started at 4:45 p.m. on Thanksgiving. On the way in, I saw a line of customers wrapped around the store, penned in by French barricades. David was inside, his back to the doors, where the first few dozen customers, their eyes hungry, waited and watched us. After a few minutes, David called all staff to the front. The day, he said, was all about efficiency: get them in and out and worry about upselling and attaching other products tomorrow. Most customers who came on Thanksgiving had a particular product, a particular sale, in mind. Help them find it and send them on their way.

Next came the inspiration part. He praised the staff and reminded everyone that they were here, yep, to have fun. I looked around, hoping to catch some rolling eyes, but my young colleagues weren't as cynical as I was. The final part of the speech was meant to address our expectations of what the night would hold: "This won't be like the YouTube videos you've seen." We had a plan, he promised, and we would never lose control of the store.

With three minutes before the doors opened, David told everyone to take their positions. At home theater, Robert handed me a stack of pages: one final change to protocol. Rather than sending customers through the line dragging their TVs behind them, we'd write down the product's name and SKU on the paper and someone would bring the item to the front after they'd checked out.

With one minute left, Anthony grabbed me and told me to stay near the accessories aisle: cables, adaptors, and wall mounts. "I want you doing simple stuff, no offense," he said. No problem, I answered, though I felt a little twinge of hurt. *You have no idea how much I've learned!* I thought. Just then, the front doors opened.

David was right: this didn't look like YouTube. The security guards were letting only a handful people through at a time. And though the customers had a look of distress and urgency on their faces as they ran through the store, there weren't enough of them to elbow each other out of the way or push each other down. They also seemed to know exactly where they were going: they had the store map ready in their head and the product they wanted, and its price, circled on a Best Buy flyer. Home theater filled up a little more slowly than the other sections, presumably because the best TV sale was a ticketed item. Eventually, though, there were more customers than I had ever seen before crowding around the 8K Samsung and pointing in wonder.

The Thanksgiving shoppers are the true diehard bargain hunters, willing to leave their families, ignore the lure of leftovers, and resist another glass of wine to go poke around the TV department of a big-box store. One refrain I heard over and over was that the markdowns didn't seem dramatic enough. Pretty much every customer I asked said that they shopped on Thanksgiving every year.

The first two hours were nonstop. I couldn't help one customer without being interrupted by three more. To walk anywhere was to invite a thousand questions. I have never said "Give me one minute" so many times in a row. I asked Luis whether this was about the size the crowd was last year, and he said it was noticeably smaller. He seemed sanguine about this fact: "Good for us, bad for the company," he said.

Eventually, the first rush began to fade. The people who had waited in line had mostly gotten what they wanted, paid, and left, though reinforcements arrived steadily. I took my scheduled dinner at 6:45, heading back to the "hub," the employee lounge, to eat a sandwich. Another home-theater guy was there, and we talked about what was moving quickly and what wasn't. He said he sold an 8K TV, which astounded me. The best I'd been able to manage was a $700 Samsung. Whereas conversation during breaks was usually about anything but Best Buy, now we were all talking about how things were going on the floor. Everyone seemed exhausted, and closing was still seven hours away.

When I got back to home theater, it turned out that the calm I had noticed was just the prelude to a second wave that began at about eight o'clock. That was when the late eaters arrived. This group had more whole families, groups of six or seven or ten who had exhausted their kitchens at home, maybe lounged on the couch and watched a bit of football, and were now ready for the evening's entertainment. These shoppers still wanted impossibly low prices, but they were more in the mood to browse for them. The pace of sales slowed down. Every now and again, as I stood talking with a customer, Sid would come by and "conversationally" remind me that we offered a 10 percent discount for anyone who signed up for the Best Buy credit card. "Chris, don't forget we offer ten percent off the already low Black Friday sales price if they sign up for a card." No, I haven't forgotten since the last time you told me, five minutes ago.

By about ten, an absolute form of weariness set in. I found it more and more tempting to return to the hub and sit down, just for five minutes, and I wasn't alone. On one visit, Luis walked in and saw about six of us sitting around with blank stares on our faces. "Everybody looks like they had enough," he said. The problem wasn't that this shift was much longer than a normal shift; it was that out on the floor, there was absolutely no down time, and even the most ingeniously designed traffic-control system couldn't fix that.

The third wave came at midnight. I'm not certain who these customers were, though the number of whole families, including toddlers, remained high. My guess was that a good number of them thought the store wouldn't open until midnight—i.e., Black Friday itself—or that somehow the deals would improve once the calendar officially ticked over one more day. At 12:45, the floor was as jammed as it had been all day, and word got around that though we would stop accepting new shoppers after 1:00 a.m., we wouldn't be kicking anyone out. Employees were expected to stay until the last customers decided to leave on their own.

Eventually, after the supply of new customers was cut off, the numbers inside the store began to dwindle. I went full half minutes without being flagged down. The store looked notably depleted: stockpiles of certain TVs had vanished, and even the less popular models were heading out the door. Overall, the system seemed to work: the lines never got super long, everyone was able to buy something, no one was killed. On the staff side, even the most egregious sale-stealers were tamed, and a cooperative spirit held. Or maybe it just felt that way because we were too tired to do anything but keep things moving along.

Shortly before closing, I bumped into David near the hub. He asked how I was holding up, and I told him I was exhausted but also somehow still fired up. He said to save some energy for tomorrow, "the real crazy time." The store would be open for seventeen hours straight, the longest shopping day of the year.

The sales floor when I arrived the next morning had been hurriedly put back together, like a drunk who has tucked in his shirt on the way to work after an all-nighter. Most of the traffic-control mechanisms were still in place, but there were gaps in the barriers now: some of the TVs and microwave boxes that formed the line to the checkout had been sold off. I saw Sid on my way back from the hub, and I asked how we did the day before. Ninety percent of the revenue target and 173 out of 200 credit card applications. "Pretty good!" I said, but he looked stricken. "We like to aim for 110 percent," he said.

I walked down the half-empty aisles. There was a feeling of picking over the bones of last night's feast, an impression only reinforced when I stumbled across a customer eating leftover turkey and mashed potatoes out of a Tupperware container in the DVD section. I flashed back to an image of the original store in Minnesota, after the tornado.

In home theater, the customers repeated some of the same questions from the night before. Was this really the sale price? Where did the doorbuster TVs go? And added a new one: Wait, you guys were open last night?

A lot of the work of the day consisted in trying to find the actual in-stock box for TVs we had already sold. I tried to make a mental note every time I saw a different model out on the floor, but more often than not the boxes moved before I had a chance to return to them. As supplies ran low, I got pretty adept at moving the giant platform ladder around (see training video #1, "Ladder Safety SOP") to grab inventory stored on the high shelves on the store's perimeter. Normally an employee in a black inventory shirt (like mine) would be "downstocking" constantly to keep items on the floor, but there was too much to keep up with.

I spent a lot of time with a couple who came in wanting a curved TV and had to work through the seven stages of grief after I told them curved TVs weren't really a thing anymore. An hour later, I saw them with Sid, and they very kindly pointed out to him that I had answered a bunch of their questions already. Sid told them not to worry about that — we weren't working on commission, so there was no need to credit me.

One customer asked me if I could help him carry a TV to his car. He was in his forties, a bit soft in the middle. With him was a woman who must have been his mother, judging by her age and her ceaseless hectoring as he attempted to lift and move the TV, a 75-inch LG, into his minivan. Our first attempt to get the box in the car left about a foot sticking out of the back. The man moved up the driver's seat and told me to do the same to the passenger side. All the while, mom was standing on the sidelines, telling her son that it would never work, that he was stupid for even trying. He didn't say anything, but I saw a kind of grim determination set in. He gave the box a big shove, and the front seats buckled a bit farther forward. Another shove, and the box started to compress. One last shove and he slammed down the tailgate, giving his mom a look of triumph and rage. I went back inside.

According to the security guards, rage was the watchword for the parking area all day. People fighting over spaces, cars nearly running over pedestrians, customers triple-parking out front to carry their purchases to their cars. At lunch, I talked to one of the guards, who said a few fistfights had broken out. The fact that none of this action made a ripple inside the store was a testament to the order we were able to impose, at least for that day.

Mealtimes were assigned again, and during my half hour I found myself at a table with Luis and Robert, though the latter seemed to be nodding off as we sat there. We talked about the day, and a vision of it from their perspective solidified for me. Black Friday wasn't something to celebrate; it was something to survive, two days of punishment that allowed for the long stretches of quiet days that pile up on either end of it. Even the weekend before Christmas Eve was easier. The job was pretty good, though, and there was even room for advancement if you wanted it. So they jumped into the melee and held their breath till they emerged from the other side.

I made one last sale that felt meaningful. A guy with long dreads looped up under a cap, a Jamaican accent, and a wispy, pointy beard told me he had a simple request: he wanted the biggest, cheapest TV he could buy. He didn't care who made it or what the technical details were: really big and really cheap. Finally a mission I could get behind. I pulled out my phone and showed him a picture of a Chinese-made 65-inch Hisense for $349. He didn't hesitate. "That's it," he said. The only problem was that there was only one left in the store, and I had no idea where it was. I hatched a plan: I'll go look in the warehouse, I told him, but there's one other place it may be. A TV this big and this cheap might be serving as a part of the checkout-line barrier. I told him to go patrol the line with an eye for the tur-quoise Hisense logo, and I'd go look in the back.

The warehouse looked a little worse for the wear after en-during the visits of a few dozen employees like me over the course of the day. To find the TVs I had to move boxes out of the way and climb over a stack of microwaves. Still, no 65-inch Hisense. I made a few loops in the back before giving up and heading to the front of the store—where, to my happy surprise, the customer was waiting with a big grin, leaning on a gigantic Hisense box.

"You found it on the line?" I asked.

"You knew it!" he said.

He gave me a fist bump. From a Best Buy perspective, it was probably all a waste of time: I would have to sell ten of those an hour to match the highest-end one in the same size.

But I got a customer exactly what he wanted, and he looked delighted. Plus, and I promise, all these TVs look the same once you get them home.

I clocked out and went to say good-bye to Terrell, Luis, and Robert. They told me to get home safe, then turned back to the customer storm. It was nine o'clock, and they still had another hour before closing. Over my career at Best Buy, I sold between $30,000 and $40,000 worth of TVs. A better seller (and this includes every single one of my colleagues) would have easily doubled that. Still, I felt a little proud of myself. I wondered if, when I gave my notice, they would look at my numbers and implore me to stay on, just a little bit longer. Then again, now that Black Friday was over, they didn't really need me anymore.

That night, I slept a KO'ed sleep. A few days later, I called the store to tell them not to schedule me for any more shifts: I had another project that was going to take up all my time. No one returned my call, but I didn't get any more shifts either.

7

Mastering the Deadline Effect: United States Air Force

Hurricane Florence was a day away from drowning the East Coast, but the airmen were at ease. The last time a hurricane had hit the United States—in fact, it was the one-two-three punch of Harvey, Irma, and Maria—almost four hundred men and women from the 621st Contingency Response Wing of the Air Force had deployed to help with the relief effort. If Florence was anything like those disasters, a lot of the people I saw walking through McGuire Air Force Base would be leaving within hours. And yet, no one looked rushed or harried. The gloomy weather made everything on the base seem like it was happening in slow motion—the giant arms of the storm had pressed clouds down on all of southern New Jersey, and the air was eerily still.

There was a reason that everyone was so calm: they were prepared. They were so prepared that they could spend hours showing me around the base without affecting in the slightest their ability to start hurricane relief the next day.

My first meeting was with Chief Master Sergeant David Abell and Colonel Ryan Marshall, the two leaders of the unit. The Contingency Response Wing does what it sounds like it does—it responds to "contingencies" like earthquakes and hurricanes, not to mention the last-second crises that can crop up in a war zone. Specifically, the 621st is a rapid-response force that can open an airfield capable of landing giant aircraft just about anywhere in the world. And for disaster relief, having a working airfield can mean the difference between life and death for people needing shelter, food, and water.

So: Abell and Marshall, two important fellows, commanders of fifteen hundred airmen in the only unit of the Air Force devoted to deploying at a moment's notice, on the eve of a storm that would keep the Carolinas underwater for weeks. But here they were, sitting down with me in their office and walking me through their operation. I told them it didn't look like anyone was about to go hop on a cargo plane and coordinate a wide-reaching relief effort, but they assured me they were poised to do just that. "We're ready," Marshall said. "We got folks here on the East Coast that are ready to go out the door when called. We are designed to go in quick, light, lethal, agile."

The standard was to be in the air—on an Air Force C-5 or C-17, big planes with the capacity to pack in a whole tent city and the means to assemble it—within twelve hours of getting a call from the Pentagon. What's more, each mission was essentially unknowable until it arrived. It could be anything from distributing food to preparing for an invasion. The approaching storm was no different. "After something like a hurricane," Abell said, "you have no idea what kind of damage has been done."

There was a lesson here for anyone facing more mundane deadlines, but it took me a while to learn it. In the meantime,

Abell was talking me through some of the 621st's most recent missions. There was a relief effort in Haiti following Hurricane Matthew, in 2016. Airfield operations near Raqqa, Syria, and Mosul, Iraq, as those two cities were being reclaimed from ISIS. (Seven members of the 621st had received Bronze Stars during those deployments.) The response to Harvey, Irma, and Maria, which had his squadrons spread over fifteen locations at the same time. In Puerto Rico, the Air Force flew 2,800 airlift missions to distribute 16 million pounds of aid. "We were heavily involved in that operation, trying to get those airfields back open," Abell said. "Because they are an island, there was not going to be ground transportation. Their ability to get supplies and relief was strictly through air."

Before I left to tour the base and meet the men and women who had pulled off those life-saving missions, Abell told me about an unusual event that would be taking place later that day. One of the airmen, Staff Sergeant Thomas Vaughn, would receive what amounted to a battlefield promotion to technical sergeant, the next rung on the ladder of ranks. Normally such promotions took months and required the airman to take a seemingly endless series of tests. In this case, though, the Air Force was cutting through all that red tape: "We have a stripe that we can give out on the spot. So we looked across our entire wing, at all of our staff sergeants and it came down to this one." At the moment, I was the only person on the base other than the senior staff who knew about the promotion. If I saw Vaughn, Abell told me, I couldn't say a word. "Don't blow it," he said, and sent me on my way.

Major Shane Hughes had a business card, which he handed me not long after we made the drive from headquarters to the warehouse where the 621st keeps everything it needs to go anywhere in the world. The card named him as the director of operations for one of the wing's four contingency response squadrons on base and listed the squadron's motto: "Adapt and Overcome."

Hughes was handsome, with close-cropped blondish hair, mid-thirties. Like almost everyone else I met at McGuire, he seemed surprisingly relaxed, given what his job was. We walked through the warehouse, and he pointed out the various pallets designated as "on alert," meaning they'd be the ones used if there were a sudden call to action. There were pallets with giant tents on them, portable showers, heaters, generators, air tanks, and boxes of MREs (the airmen had recently celebrated the addition of Skittles to these meals). Giant bladders filled with potable water, other bladders filled with jet fuel. A collapsible trailer that could serve as an operations center with satellite communications. Hughes said that everything mechanical was built to run on jet fuel, or just about any fuel you throw at it. The last thing they want is an engine that gets fussy about what you put in it. Once a week, every pallet was checked to make sure it was still ready to go.

Outside there were Ford F-350s and Humvees painted olive drab, and giant forklifts with oversize tires meant to operate on uneven terrain. A relief operation is essentially a logistics job — like Best Buy on Black Friday, if there were a significantly higher chance of flying debris or bullets killing the truck drivers and forklift operators. The members of the 621st were trained to work under any lighting conditions, including with night-vision goggles during complete blackout. I asked how they could drive a forklift in the pitch black. "Very, very slowly," Hughes said. Everything, from the vehicles to the stacks of MREs, was sized to fit on one of the three planes the 621st uses, the C-5, the C-17, or the C-130.

While we were inspecting the gear, two of Hughes's men joined us. Sergeants Ronald Rowe and Donald Wheeland had both been with the 621st when the unit deployed to Haiti after

Hurricane Matthew, in 2016. Matthew was a Category 4 hurricane when it made landfall, the strongest storm to hit Haiti since 1964. For a country still reeling from the 2010 earthquake, it was a devastating blow. More than 200,000 homes were damaged, 546 people died, and nearly 1.4 million were in need of aid. The Haitian government called Washington, and the Pentagon called up the 621st. Within fourteen hours they were on the ground in Port-au-Prince. "I was on one of the first trucks," Rowe said.

Rowe and Wheeland walked me through what happened once they got word that they were flying south. It wasn't what I expected. To start, the men and women who were deploying didn't pack their bags, they didn't start assembling information about their mission, they didn't run around making sure everything got loaded onto a cargo plane. Instead, they went home, where their bags were already packed—every squadron on alert keeps their bags ready to go—and they spent some time with their husbands, wives, children, girlfriends, and boyfriends.

Hughes explained: "Once we get that deployment order, we're all going home to make sure that everything is lined up with our families, that all the bills are going to get paid. All those little things that if you're going to be gone for sixty days, that's all taken care of." Being part of a unit that can be called away at any time is stressful enough—this at least allows for a proper good-bye. Keeping the families happy was just as important to overall morale as taking care of the airmen themselves.

Back on base, a mission planning cell, made up of airmen who weren't deploying, was doing all the prep work. That included communicating with the Haitian government, gathering intel on the state of the local infrastructure, and preparing to bring in whatever the situation required. The Port-au-Prince airport was still usable, so the focus was on setting up a system to get as many planes of relief supplies on the ground, unloaded, and back in the air as quickly as possible. As the clock wound down toward the end of the twelve-hour deployment window, the airmen came back on base and got a full briefing from the mission planning cell.

"Basically they hand us all of the information, the contacts, everything that they've got when we're on our way out the door," Hughes said. "Then, they'll keep working even after we're gone to get more information, so that whenever we land, our in-boxes just explode with good info." Rowe and Wheeland said that once they arrived in Haiti, they set to work almost at once to build a new helicopter landing pad: there wasn't room to land airplanes and helicopters at the same time, so they had to improvise.

Food started arriving from abroad in military and civilian aircraft, which the 621st loaded onto helicopters that flew to some of the hardest-hit areas, places where every tree had been shorn of its leaves. "We started loading helicopters with bags of rice, as much as they could handle," Rowe said. "I think we were busting their capacity sometimes." All the while, the rest of the 621st was setting up tents so the unit could feed and shelter the airmen now stationed in Haiti for an indefinite amount of time.

Occasionally, Rowe and Wheeland would board the helicopters themselves and help distribute the bags of rice. Wheeland wasn't given to naked expressions of sentiment, but his voice softened when he remembered this hand-to-hand interaction with the Haitians. "That was one of the rewarding things," he said, "to see that it was actually going to people who really needed it." I was reminded of what Rebecca Solnit said about the feeling of shared purpose that arose following a natural disaster: it was "an emotion graver than happiness but deeply positive."

The 621st stayed on the ground in Port-au-Prince for fourteen days. And then they did the whole operation in reverse. "After fourteen days, you just pack everything up, put it back on the plane, and fly it back here?" I asked.

"Yes," said Rowe, and all three of the airmen laughed.

"We come back and we have a reconstitution period," Hughes said, "so that we can get the equipment back to one hundred percent as fast as possible and then we can set ourselves back up to go and do it again."

The phrase the airmen use to describe the squadron that's next to deploy is "sitting on alert," and that seems to capture the spirit of that time spent on base. They're so ready, they're at rest.

Each squadron spends three months of each year on alert. Wheeland told me his girlfriend loved those three months because it was when they got to spend the most time together. Airmen on alert have to remain close to the base, and they are exempt from any of the off-site training exercises that fill up the rest of the year.

The flip side of that is the possibility that they'll be called away. Hughes, Rowe, and Wheeland were all sitting on alert when we spoke—more than anyone at headquarters, they were the ones who might have to upend their lives for Florence—and they were the calmest trio on the base. Not that the storm wasn't on their minds. "Yesterday, I got a text from my dad," Rowe said. "He was like, 'Are you all getting ready to leave?' Because they're all watching the news and they know what we do at this point. I told him, 'I don't know, when I get the word, I'll get the word. I'll let you know.'"

I asked if that combination, of being both most and least likely to be available on any given day, was hard on their families. Rowe said it was. One thing he had learned was to always warn his parents to get travel insurance if they were coming to visit him. There was no telling when the next earthquake might hit, or whether that tropical depression might turn into a full-fledged monster.

Hughes told me that his sister had come to visit him three times at McGuire. "She's seen my wife all three times," he said, "and she has seen me once, for one of the days. When I'm on alert, they know there is a good chance it's going to be a family visit minus me."

If the 621st is the Air Force's vanguard response unit, Alpha Mike is the vanguard of the vanguard. They are the advance team that deploys before all the rest to assess whatever airfield the unit is planning to use and make sure it can handle that first cargo plane — and every one after it. Whereas the 621st has the capability to send hundreds of men and women to a disaster, Alpha Mike is always the same size: eight airmen, each an expert in one part of what's needed to determine if an airfield is ready to receive heavy traffic.

Shane Hughes called Alpha Mike "our lighter and leaner first group of responders" as he walked me over to the hangar where they were based. Their alert package is much smaller: two Humvees loaded with supplies and two all-terrain vehicles called MRZRs ("em-razors") for navigating in areas that the Humvees can't go. It's made to fit on the smallest of the planes the 621st uses.

Six members of Alpha Mike were waiting to meet us. I called Rowe and Wheeland the calmest men on base, but that's just what I had in my notebook until I met this crew. In their casual camaraderie, they resembled a kickball team more than a military unit. To describe them as calm would imply that they were aware of a threat somewhere on the horizon. (Florence who?)

Hughes introduced me to the officer in charge, Major Allen Jennings. He was skinny, with a flop of hair shaved close around the ears. Before I could ask him a question, Jennings announced that rather than talking in the hangar, we were going to go for a ride in the MRZRs. I was handed a motorcycle helmet (on missions they use combat helmets) and a pair of waterproof fatigues. There might be some mud along the way, Jennings warned me, but "we're going to try to keep the vehicle upright."

The MRZR looked like a supercharged, battle-hardened golf cart. Like everything else the 621st uses, it runs on jet fuel. We climbed in, four to a golf cart, and sped off. My driver, as it turned out, was Sergeant Vaughn, the airman who would be receiving a surprise promotion that day. He had dark, slicked-back hair, like Brando in *The Wild One*, if you replaced all of Brando's rebel attitude with aw-shucks earnestness. I was tempted to find out if he knew what was coming, but the MRZR's engine was so loud we could barely talk.

Vaughn drove us past barracks and hospitals and tarmacs filled with cargo planes. McGuire is part of a joint base with Fort Dix, which belongs to the Army, and soon we entered their territory. The only thing that changed were the fatigues on the men and women we saw.

We turned off the paved road onto a gravel one that led into the trees: the base is big enough to include hundreds of acres of forest, which the army uses for combat training. After about fifteen minutes, we left the gravel road for no road. It looked like we were plunging randomly into the underbrush. That was the point—Jennings wanted to prove that the MRZR was nimble enough to weave through, over, or under just about any obstacle, whether it was a downed tree, a steep incline, or a pool of soupy mud. We stayed upright, though at times just barely.

We stopped when we reached a clearing, and Vaughn pulled off his helmet. A shock of hair fell into his eyes. "Hey," he said, "since you work at *GQ*, do you know if there's a pomade that will stand up to a helmet?" (I did not.) Meanwhile, the whole team had assembled around Jennings. "We figured this would be a better place to talk than back on base," he said. First, he walked me through the eight members of the team. Really, though, it was seven plus one: the regular members of Alpha

Mike, plus a high-ranking officer pulled from elsewhere in the Air Force to handle on-the-ground talks with the local government. That officer had to be an O-6 or above, which meant a colonel or a general.

The others were chosen for their ability to do the work of getting an airfield up and running with the smallest crew possible. There was an operations officer to handle air traffic control, two civil engineers to test the hardiness of the runway, a communications specialist to make sure they could send information back to McGuire and the Pentagon, a cargo specialist or "aerial porter" who was an expert in logistics, and a single member of the security forces, who was more heavily armed than the rest and kept the whole operation safe. Vaughn was security for Alpha Mike—he called himself the team's "cop."

After Hurricane Maria hit Puerto Rico, an Alpha Mike team was sent to the island to figure out which airports could support relief missions. San Juan airport was usable—and supplies did come in that way—but the Pentagon didn't want to get in the way of civilian flights. (Before and after the storm, as many as 400,000 Puerto Ricans left the island.) Attention quickly turned to a decommissioned naval base called Roosevelt Roads about 40 miles east of San Juan. The only problem was that it hadn't seen heavy traffic since the Navy turned it over to civilian control in 2004. Alpha Mike's job was to go to Roosevelt Roads and see if its runways were ready to handle the arrival of approximately 40,000 pounds of cargo an hour, 24 hours a day.

Once the team landed in Puerto Rico, they got to work. The communications officer set up a link with the mainland, the operations officer took over the existing air traffic control tower (though they have the ability to set up their own, portable tower), security checked the perimeter, the O-6 went to do whatever it is colonels do, and the two engineers began testing the tarmac. That involved drilling dozens of holes all along the runway, taking core samples, and analyzing whatever data they could collect. The goal was to determine not just how big a plane could safely land at the airfield, but how many total takeoffs and landings the strip could handle before it fell apart. A million pounds of cargo a day will beat up just about any airport.

Four hours. That's the amount of time Alpha Mike has on the ground to deliver its assessment back to base before the bigger crews start arriving. Jennings described that window as "tight," the first admission I'd heard from anyone on the base that what they do is incredibly tricky. To pull it off, he said, they have to go "all the way to the walls." Often the pace is so demanding that the team doesn't have time to unpack their tents and bedding, so they sleep on the ramp. "Uncomfortable is normal," Jennings said. "Uncomfortable is expected."

I asked Jennings how he kept his team ready for these missions, to be the first to deploy, and with the least amount of information about what awaited them. Well, he said, they had no choice. If the call could come at any moment, procrastination was impossible. So they checked and rechecked their equipment. They packed their bags. They went for joyrides in MRZRs. They practiced each element of a deployment, segment by segment, then practiced the full run. "It's the reps of doing something that count," he said. "So that when they step out the door to go do it for real, while the place may be new, the thing they're doing is routine."

For a while, I thought the 621st was going to serve as an example of the power of using all the strategies I had learned about handling deadlines at once. They made ample use of self-imposed deadlines, for one, and they had made themselves experts at the kind of interdependent teamwork I saw at Best Buy, at the Fulton, and on the Easter lily farm. They ran numerous training exercises, which often felt indistinguishable from the real thing—a soft deadline with teeth that was similar to what I saw at Telluride. They revised in response to facts on the ground, like when they built a helicopter landing pad on the spot in Haiti. And they were experts at focusing their mission, right down to optimizing for team size and getting the airfield opened safely before worrying about, say, how comfy their beds would be that night.

But it wasn't until I came across a few publications by an economist at MIT named Muhamet Yildiz that I truly understood what made the 621st's work possible. Yildiz had published a working paper called "Optimism, Deadline Effect, and Stochastic Deadlines," which was about the negative version of the deadline effect, the one that leads to negotiations dragging on until the last possible minute.

Yildiz found, however, that this deadline effect disappears if the deadline is "stochastic," which is just a fancy way of saying "random." If, for example, the MTA and the transit workers' union were told they had to have a new contract before the next major track fire (which occur frequently but unpredictably and which require extra labor to get under control), they would have the necessary combination of importance and randomness to strike a deal without waiting for a specific deadline. (Yildiz also pointed me to a study of eBay and Amazon auctions that showed that last-minute bidding decreased and winning bids were placed earlier when the ending time for the auction was allowed to float rather than remain fixed.)

"By imposing a deadline that is triggered by an event that will happen at a random time and is beyond the parties' control," Yildiz wrote, the deadline effect could be tamed. The reason for this is fairly intuitive: if you think you might run out of bargaining time at any moment, you'll be more likely to compromise.

Alpha Mike and the rest of the 621st were pointing toward the psychic and practical benefits of that approach. They faced deadlines that were fully stochastic: natural disasters that could strike anywhere, and at any time. And yet they seemed to live a life that was somehow both high-stakes and stress-free. If you think you may be called to show your cards at any moment, you're more likely to always be holding a strong hand. (One could make the same argument about life itself. It is, after all, an assignment with a stochastic deadline.)

As a group, they had achieved what the psychologist Mihaly Csikszentmihalyi called "flow"—the relish you feel when you have been stretched to your limits to accomplish a difficult and worthwhile goal. In his book on the subject, Csikszentmihalyi quotes a dancer, who describes how it feels when a performance is going well: "Your concentration is very complete. Your mind isn't wandering, you are not thinking of something else; you are totally involved in what you are doing. . . . You feel relaxed, comfortable, and energetic." A person experiencing flow, Csikszentmihalyi wrote, "need not fear unexpected events, or even death."

Now, not everyone can count on a natural disaster to keep them on their toes. But there's a way to mimic everything else—the exercises, the scheduled check-ins, the day-by-day work of never falling behind—to achieve the same effect. After all, even Alpha Mike didn't need the hurricane to actually *land* to achieve their state of readiness.

Florence, for what it's worth, didn't do the type of damage that required the help of the 621st. There was death and flooding and toxic spills, but the government didn't need to call in the relief units of the Air Force. Jennings and Vaughn and all the rest stayed home. But they were ready all the same.

By the time we arrived back from the MRZR tour, most of the squadron had assembled at Alpha Mike's hangar. Vaughn looked baffled: only Sergeant Abell and three others knew what was in store—the airmen had been told to gather for an announcement and that's it. Sergeant Vaughn walked over and got in formation with all the rest.

There was a brief break in the clouds, and sunlight blasted through the hangar door as Abell and Marshall walked in to address the men and women. They said that ever since they had taken command of the 621st, they regretted that they were stuck on base while the rest of the unit got to go out into the field. "You get to do the cool stuff," Marshall said. "You literally get to save lives." It wasn't all dreariness back at headquarters, though. Occasionally the Department of Defense gave them an opportunity to do something special.

Recently, the Air Force had been told to increase the number of promotions that commanders could give out on the spot, through a program called STEP: Stripes for Exceptional Performers. (Everything in the military, no matter how wonderful, had to be given a dull and impenetrable acronym.) They asked the airmen if they had ever heard of a STEP promotion—and they admitted they had, though no one had ever seen one in person. Well, they said, we're going to do one today: "Staff Sergeant Vaughn, please step forward." A hoot went up among the crowd.

"Son," the commander said, "this is about to change your life." He pulled the insignia for Staff Sergeant—four stripes around a star—off Vaughn's arm and put one with five stripes in its place. Vaughn was now a technical sergeant. Someone handed him a bottle of champagne. The whole squadron cheered, before chanting "Speech! Speech!" ("I've never been part of a unit that every single person cares about you," Vaughn said, "and the CRW is like that.")

Afterward, Jennings told me the whole process—from getting Pentagon approval to bringing in Vaughn's family—had come together, like seemingly everything else the 621st did, in twelve hours. "It's literally like a World War Two battlefield promotion," he said. He still seemed shocked at what had happened, which gives one a sense of how arduous the normal route for a promotion must be. I found Rowe and Wheeland standing nearby and asked them what they thought. "It's very motivational," Wheeland said, to which Jennings added, "It's motivational when you see the right people getting it."

I had assumed that the STEP promotion would be a charming thing to witness but essentially unrelated to any deadline wisdom I might cull from the 621st. Talking to Rowe and Wheeland, however, I realized that I was wrong. This was another sort of stochastic deadline, a random but powerful force that had the effect of motivating the entire squadron. A promotion, it seemed, could come at any time, as long as you were operating at a high enough level.

In some sense, every time we face a deadline we are attempting to use urgency to spur action. The tactics that businesses use to meet their deadlines or motivate their workers are a way of reapportioning that urgency: by moving up deadlines, by breaking them up into shorter chunks, by focusing the mission, by making teams interdependent. The trick is to feel that deadline effect constantly, even when the deadline itself has disappeared.

The joke that Cyril Parkinson made in *The Economist* in 1955—"Work expands so as to fill the time available for its completion"—is also a sort of life sentence for the office drudge. But what if we tried to escape this tyranny? What if we were so ready for anything, we could be relaxed about everything? Wouldn't this state begin to look less like being on deadline and more like being at peace?

Epilogue

This book had a deadline. It was March 1, 2020. When you sign a book contract, you get to set the date you want to turn it in and, having already read Elizabeth Martin's census study, I chose the earliest date I felt comfortable putting down on paper. I had one year to report, write, and revise the book before sending it to the publisher.

The first hurdle I had to overcome was something my editor, Ben Loehnen, said shortly after the contract was signed. He told me about a different writer he was working with who had called him in a panic when she missed her delivery date. Ben, kindly, told the writer not to worry—he didn't even keep track of the official deadline, as long as a writer didn't go *too* far past it. This was apparently the norm in book publishing, but it was absolutely fatal to anyone, like me, hoping to harness a deadline to work quickly.

I had seen what the flexibility of book deadlines had done to Robert Caro, author of *The Power Broker* and four volumes of a planned five-volume biography of Lyndon Johnson. He had begun his career in the newspaper business and had once been able to turn around a story in a matter of hours. "When I turned to writing books," he wrote, "the deadlines were no longer at the end of a day, or a week, or, occasionally, if you were lucky in journalism, a month. They were years away. But there *were* deadlines: the publisher's delivery dates. And there was another constraint: money—money to live on while I was doing the research. But the hard truth was that for me neither of these constraints could stand before the force of this other thing." The other thing, he explains, was the desire to keep researching and reporting before starting to write. He's been working on his LBJ books for almost fifty years now.

Ben Loehnen and Robert Caro: these people were my enemies. My book was due on March 1, and I was going to have a finished book by March 1. I started with a bit of right-to-left planning. One of my first interviews was with Bill West, and I remembered a warning he gave me. "People try to get too detailed instead of building a top-level schedule," he said. Figure out the big stuff first and fill in the details later. I knew I needed to finish all of the reporting by the end of the year, and I wanted as little overlap between chapters as possible. So I made a simple calendar: two workplaces in the spring, three in the summer, three in the fall. (My reporting from Telluride also took place in the fall, but I had written that chapter already—it was part of the book proposal that got me the contract in the first place.)

I set up self-imposed deadlines for the chapters themselves, which would serve as checkpoints along the way. I would write up each one after I had finished reporting and then set it aside. By the end of May, for example, I had a full draft of the chapter on Jean-Georges Vongerichten and the Fulton. There was even a sort of publishing version of a friends and family meal, when an excerpt of the restaurant chapter appeared in *The New York Times Magazine*. At the Fulton, the risotto was taken off the menu that night. In the *Times Magazine*, the Paris Café was mostly relegated to the cutting-room floor.

My original proposal had nine chapters: the plan was for Airbus and the Public Theater to be their own case studies. By mid-summer, however, it was clear that I'd have to focus my mission. Airbus's new assembly line for the A220 wouldn't be up and running for another year. And the behind-the-scenes look at David Cale's show, while fascinating, worked best in a supporting rather than lead role. So, like John Delaney abandoning his fifty-state bus tour, I turned nine chapters into seven.

We're getting now into the home stretch. After the reporting was done, I did something unusual: I took on a new day job, as an editor at the *New York Times*. I had been reading a lot of social science papers, and I remembered something Joseph Heath and Joel Anderson had written in "Procrastination and the Extended Will": "the best way to ensure that one is working at a reasonably high intensity level is to take on too much." Perhaps I was also thinking of the Viennese writer Karl Kraus, who claimed, "A journalist is stimulated by a deadline. He writes worse when he has time." Each morning, I would arrive at work two hours before everyone else. Those would be my two hours to work on the book, which lent an undeniable focus to my labors. In case you think I'm coming across as too robotically disciplined, I should add that I was fairly exhausted with this schedule by the end of it.

By the new year, I had established a soft open for myself, and I had given it teeth. I resolved that I would finish the book by the second week in February. To make sure that I followed through, I told my wife, Georgia, and my agent, Chris

Parris-Lamb, I would be sending it to them that week. At this point, I made an error. I thought to myself: I'll try to send them everything, but it's okay if I just send them the body of the book and keep working on the introduction and conclusion. (How could I, after all, be writing these words if I sent them everything?) Sure enough, February arrived and I was able to send over only the body of the book.

Still, the soft deadline set me up to have everything done by March 1. With Chris and Georgia and, eventually, Ben as my preview audience, I was able to revise what I had: cut from here, add a new song there, work on my showstoppers.

And, finally, from the moment I signed that contract, the whole arrangement was one of reciprocal interdependence. Ben couldn't start editing until I delivered the book; I couldn't start revising until Ben got his comments back to me; the copy editor and fact-checker and production editor and publicity team were waiting on all of us. We were like Alpha Mike, but with fewer sidearms. It was a giant, animated, high-powered deadline machine, and who was I to gum up the works?

Here's the twist: March 1 arrived. I had a book that I thought was ready. But I couldn't get that first conversation with Ben about the flexible delivery date out of my head. So, at the very end of the process, I asked Ben if I could have another month, just to let it sit for a while, and he said yes. After all, we had set the deadline so early—there was no rush.

Michael Pollan began his book *In Defense of Food* with this advice: "Eat food. Not too much. Mostly plants." If I had to summarize this book in seven words, I might choose: "Set a deadline, the earlier the better." (Yes, Pollan's is catchier.) Those two ideas are behind every successful organization we've studied here. The deadline provides the engine; moving it early allows you to steer the car.

We can see the evidence everywhere. On the crowdfunding platform Kickstarter, projects with the maximum time limit of sixty days are considerably less successful than projects with shorter deadlines. At Microsoft, an experimental program to limit the workweek to four days led to a 40 percent increase in productivity. In New Zealand, a similar plan also led to increased productivity—and a big jump in workers' happiness.

After a year spent in the field, that was the lesson that hit home the hardest. Deadlines, time management, productivity: these aren't just abstractions for economists to study. They determine the material conditions of our lives.

It was impossible to understand the workplaces I visited without glimpsing the larger economic and social world they were a part of. Thus Linda Crockett taught me how to force an Easter lily to bloom, but she also couldn't stop talking about immigration policy and the death of the family farm. Telluride's opening day required a team of snowmakers, which turned a skiing story into a climate-change story. Best Buy had mastered Black Friday, but across town Macy's was shuttering stores and eliminating 2,000 jobs nationwide. I could talk electoral tactics with John Delaney, but the farmers of Iowa wanted to talk socialism and health care with him.

Almost fifty years ago, John McPhee wrote an article for *The New Yorker* called "The Search for Marvin Gardens." One thread of the story, as you might expect, was about Monopoly. McPhee wrote about playing the game, and he went to Atlantic City to track down where the names of the various properties had come from. There were Boardwalk and Park Place, Ventnor and St. Charles. A friend of mine called that part of the article Story A. As McPhee drove around the Jersey Shore, though, past boarded-up homes and broken windows, a second theme emerged: the decline of the American city. When McPhee finally finds Marvin Gardens, he discovers it's not even in Atlantic City. It is, as he writes, "a suburb within a suburb." That was Story B.

For the organizations I studied while reporting this book, Story B was often dire. Workers were under considerable pressure, even before the coronavirus pandemic upended the economy. We were and are in a time of disruption, displacement, and frustration. And yet, Story A, the one where we see people just doing their jobs, was one punctuated by joy and humor. The workers I met didn't always know what the future would hold, but they knew that, today, they were on schedule and doing okay.

McPhee himself confessed to a significant amount of anxiety when it came to writing. Each day, he said, he would go to the office and hem and haw, panic and procrastinate, check his notes and rearrange his desk. But then, finally, by the end of the day, when he couldn't avoid it any more, he'd get a few more words down on the page. "The routine of doing this six days a week puts a little drop in a bucket each day, and that's the key," he said. "Because if you put a drop in a bucket every day, after three hundred and sixty-five days, the bucket's going to have some water in it."

On my reporting trip out to see the Easter lilies in Smith River, I arrived late at night at a motel near the airport in Medford, Oregon. At the front desk, the clerk had just come on duty for the graveyard shift. He hadn't even put on his uniform shirt yet. He asked me what I was doing there all the way from New York and I told him.

He was a writer, too, he said. He had written ten chapters of a fantasy novel about halflings and paladins, but he was stuck now. A few years ago, he woke up in the middle of the night with a perfect vision of the final chapter, which he wrote down feverishly in the dark. But now that he had written the end, he couldn't get motivated to fill in the middle.

The answer was simple. "Set a deadline," I told him. "The earlier the better." And he promised to do just that.

Acknowledgments

I want to thank the many people who made it possible for me to write this book. My agent, Chris Parris-Lamb, shepherded the project from the very beginning, when my pitch was hardly more sophisticated than "I just want to say one word to you: deadlines." His colleagues Sarah Bolling and Will Roberts joined us shortly after that, and they have been indispensable at getting *The Deadline Effect* out into the world.

My standards for what constitutes good editing are impossibly high, but Ben Loehnen exceeded them nonetheless. He made *The Deadline Effect* so much better, chapter by chapter and sentence by sentence. I was helped in countless ways by the whole team at Avid Reader Press: Jessica Chin, Alison Forner, Morgan Hoit, Elizabeth Hubbard, Carolyn Kelly, Allie Lawrence, Amanda Mulholland, and Alexandra Primiani. Kyle Paoletta fact-checked the book and caught a nonzero number of errors.

Portions of the chapter about Jean-Georges Vongerichten's restaurants appeared in *The New York Times Magazine.* I'm grateful to Claire Gutierrez, Bill Wasik, and Jake Silverstein for asking smart questions and cutting some of my dumber jokes (while leaving a few intact). Robert Liguori fact-checked the article and caught a nonzero number of errors.

If I could, I'd list every friend who listened to me talk about this book here, but I'll single out a few who made discrete and concrete contributions. Rivka Galchen tipped me off to the story of Évariste Galois. Gideon Lewis-Kraus came up with the Story A/Story B schema. John Jeremiah Sullivan is the most fun pain-in-the-ass to edit, which produced useful material for the introduction. Several friends helped me find places to write, in one way or another: Chris Beha, Ryan Carr, Alison Cool, Willing Davidson, Deirdre Foley-Mendelssohn, Rafil Kroll-Zaidi, Jim Nelson.

I had the support of several institutions and fellowships while I was reporting and writing *The Deadline Effect*. I'm grateful to Robert Boynton and Ted Conover for giving me a home at New York University's Arthur L. Carter Journalism Institute. To Melanie C. Locay at the New York Public Library, for finding me a spot in the Frederick Lewis Allen Memorial Room, where I wrote the bulk of this book. And to Zan Strumfeld, Carly Willsie, and Josh Friedman at the Logan Nonfiction Program. The Logan fellowship allowed me to finish the book ahead of schedule, which is a good look for someone writing about deadlines.

Everyone mentioned by name in the book has my sincere gratitude for talking to me so generously and insightfully. A few others worked behind the scenes to make the reporting on each of the organizations possible: Lauren Anderson, Monica Biddix, Josh Constine, Ahmed Elsayed, Laurie Eustis, Rachel Potucek, and Elise Reinemann. Matthew Dean Marsh and Dominic Lake provided useful background on the worlds of musical theater and stylish restaurants, respectively. Special thanks to Nancy Clark for being the world's best guide to Telluride.

Finally, I'd like to thank my family for a lifetime of support: my mother and father, Suzanne, Tommy, and all six of my siblings. All my love to Carson and Alice, for inspiring me every day. And to Georgia, most of all, for everything.

Index

About the Author

Christopher Cox has written about politics, business, books, and science for *The New York Times Magazine*, *GQ*, *Harper's*, *Wired*, and *Slate*. In 2020, he was named a Knight Science Journalism Fellow at MIT and a visiting scholar at NYU's Arthur L. Carter Journalism Institute. He was formerly the chief editor of *Harper's Magazine* and executive editor of *GQ*, where he worked on stories that won the Pulitzer Prize, the PEN Literary Award for Journalism, and multiple National Magazine Awards. He lives in Brooklyn with his wife, Georgia, and their two daughters, Carson and Alice.